Copyright © The Tonford Fly Fishing Club

All Rights Reserved. No part of this book may be reproduced, stored or transmitted in any form without the prior permission in writing of the publisher.

Published in London, the United Kingdom, in 2021 by the Tonford Fly Fishing Club.

ISBN: 978-1-3999-2586-0

This book is based on the minutes and paper files of the Tonford Fly Fishing Club 1951-2021 and interviews and correspondence with individuals, clubs, government agencies and companies. The author has made every effort to confirm the accuracy of the content.

Seventy Years Fly Fishing the Great Stour:

The History of the Tonford Fly Fishing Club 1951-2021

Norman H T Parkinson

London, 2021

Tonford Fly Fishing Club

Acknowledgements

I acknowledge with thanks the assistance of: Mr Durgendra Ale; Mr Simon Chandler; The Canterbury City Council; The Canterbury and District Angling Association; the late Dr Jack Cohen; Mrs Zeena Cohen; Mr John Dawson; Mr Stuart Elgar; Mr Mark Evans; Mr Timothy Greenfield; Mr Mark Hobday; Mr Steve Hyland; Mr Gary Lagdon; Mr Iain McDonald; Mrs Margaret Parkinson; Mr Anthony Pound; Mr Neil Rogers; Mrs Suzi Ross Browne; Mr Michael Sixsmith; Mr Steven Smith; Mr Nelson Stringer; Mr Ciprian Vasiliu; Mr Anthony Wynn, and many others.

I am grateful to the late Commander Walter Smith, former Secretary and Treasurer of the Club, whose excellent meeting minutes made my task easier than it might have been.

Foreword
by Mr Mark Evans, President of the Tonford Fly Fishing Club

I am so pleased to write the foreword to this wonderful new book about our club written by Norman Parkinson. There was a real danger that much of the TFFC's history would have been lost. Norman has ensured that our story so far is preserved for the future.

I was very excited when the possibility of purchasing a stretch of the Stour came up in 2010, and my association with the river has given me much enjoyment and fellowship over the last decade.

The story of our club and its very survival is intimately bound up with a handful of farsighted and dedicated individuals. You will read about the debt we owe to these men in the pages that follow, but I must mention our founder Harry Orr, who established the club; Michael Ross Browne, who managed to keep the club going during difficult times, and Jack Cohen, a great enthusiast and protector of the club. I knew Jack well and it is very sad that he died before this book could be published.

We also owe a debt of gratitude to the SFA, who have always been exemplary waterlords.

The club is now under excellent stewardship. Chairman Gary Lagdon's knowledge and enthusiasm has really transformed the club and the fishing.

The Stour is a wonderful river, and we are all very lucky to be able to fish it whenever we want. On a sunny day, when the birds are singing and the fish are rising, it is truly a paradise.

Mark Evans

Contents

Acknowledgements	4
Foreword by the Club President	5
Contents	7
Officers of the Tonford Fly Fishing Club	10
Chapter One: The Tonford Fly Fishing Section	11
Chapter Two: The Evolution of the Club's Fishery	24
Chapter Three: The Club's Waters	44
Chapter Four: Fish, Fishing, Flies and Weeds	65
Chapter Five: Pollution, Poaching and Boating	83
Chapter Six: The Club and its Waters in the Media	99
Chapter Seven: The Tonford Fly Fishing Club Today	102

Appendices:

The Original Club Rules and Byelaws	109
Beat Maps	112
Source of Photographs	114

Officers of the Tonford Fly Fishing Club

President

1954 Air Vice-Marshal Hugh Fraser CB
1962 No President
1975 Mrs Hester Fraser
1984 No President
2021 Mr Mark Evans

Chairman

1951 Dr Harry Orr OBE
1994 Mr Michael Ross Browne
2007 Dr Jack Cohen
2014 Rev. Grahame Whittlesea
2019 Mr Gary Lagdon

Secretary

1951 Cmdr. Walter Smith RN
1961 Cmdr. Alexander Blackley Goble RN (pro tem)
1961 Cmdr. Walter Smith RN
1965 Cmdr. Alexander Blackley Goble RN
1966 Cmdr. Alexander Blackley Goble RN (with Mr Peter Holt)
1967 Mr Peter Holt
1973 Mr John Lovatt
1981 Mr Timothy Greenfield
1994 Mr Charles Jardine
1996 Dr Jack Cohen

2006 Dr Jack Cohen (with Mr Patrick Wheeler)
2007 Mr Neil Jones
2009 Mr Anthony Pound
2020 Mr Neil Rogers

Treasurer

1954 Cmdr. Alexander Blackley Goble RN
1965 Cmdr. Walter Smith RN
1974 Mr Richard Tuttle
1987 Mr Neil Williams
1994 Mr John Dawson
2004 Mr Lester Thompson
2015 Mr Ivor Pattenden
2016 Mr Anthony Pound
2019 Mr Simon Chandler

Chapter One

The Tonford Fly Fishing Section - the Foundation of the Club

The Tonford Fly Fishing Club owes its foundation to the actions of five men: Mr J L Cooke of Denton; Dr Harry Orr of Canterbury; Major J B Thompson of Barham; land-owner Air Vice-Marshall Hugh Fraser CB of Twyford, Hampshire, and Kensington, London, and, unwittingly, a miscreant river frontager named Griffiths.

In 1949, what is now known as the Tonford length of the Great Stour, from the Milton Bridge to the West of Canterbury, was owned by Major (George) Algernon Meakin, the Village Squire of Barham. He lived at Dane Chantry, Petham. Meakin was a descendant of the Burton-on-Trent brewery firm of that name. Thompson, Cooke, and Orr fished this length with Meakin's permission. It is not clear whether they had a lease or a licence or whether it was just an amicable arrangement. When Meakin died in 1949, the ownership of the land, and the fishing rights, passed to his nephew, Air Vice-Marshall Hugh Henry Macleod Fraser CB.

In his youth, Hugh Fraser was a pioneering aviator, and a member of the Royal Aero Club while studying at Cambridge. In the First World War he joined the Royal Flying Corps as a pilot, flying fighters and bombers on the Western Front. After the war he took a commission in the newly formed Royal Air Force, serving in the UK and overseas, reaching the lofty rank of Air Vice-Marshal. In the Second World War he was appointed First Director of Military Cooperation, then Director General, Repair and Maintenance, Ministry of Aircraft Production. In the 1943 King's Birthday Honours he was appointed a Companion of the Order of the Bath by King George VI. He retired in 1945. At the time of his death, he was a councillor with Winchester RDC. Both AVM Fraser and Mrs Hester Fraser would in turn become President of the club.

Air Vice-Marshall Hugh Henry Macleod Fraser (1895-1962) at age 20

Thompson, Cooke, and Orr were anxious to continue to fish the stretch, so Major Thompson approached AVM Fraser in the hope of coming to an agreement. Fraser asked for £120 per year rent (equal to over £4,000 in 2021) plus the appointment of a river keeper, annual stocking with trout, and the controlling of coarse fish. This was substantially more than the three had envisaged.

All three were members of the Canterbury and District Angling Association (CDAA) and Cooke, who would become Chairman of the CDAA from 1959 to 1975, suggested that they should formally approach the CDAA to take the lease. However, the CDAA was unwilling to take on the burden on behalf of all of its 476 members, many of whom were not fly fishers. Instead, it proposed that a semi-autonomous self-funding section might be formed within the Canterbury Association to do so. This was to become the **Canterbury and District Angling Association Tonford Fly Fishing Section** (TFFS). It was envisaged that twenty-five members would be recruited from within the CDAA, and each would pay an additional £10 for the privilege of fly fishing the Tonford water. While the CDAA did not want to take on the Tonford length for its entire membership, it was nevertheless supportive of the new Section and agreed to be a party to the lease, underwrite the first year's rent, fund operations to a maximum of £250, and to put the water under the purview of its new bailiff, Mr Smith. Air Vice-Marshall Fraser was initially happy with this arrangement, and it was agreed that the lease should be drawn up.

The CDAA set up a Sub-Committee to draft the Rules and Byelaws of the new section. This founding Sub-Committee was made up of Cooke and Commander Walter Smith RN who were both members of the CDAA Management Committee, plus Dr Orr who was an ordinary CDAA member. At its first meeting on April 1st, 1951, the Sub-Committee elected Dr Orr as its Chairman and Commander Smith as Secretary. The draft Rules were approved by both the CDAA Management Committee and Air Vice-Marshal Fraser. The Rules provided that in future there should be two members nominated by the CDAA Management Committee and three elected by the TFFS at its Annual General Meeting. So, what we now know as the Tonford Fly Fishing Club started as a section of the CDAA.

The early club Minutes meticulously present members' titles and rank in an interesting reflection of the time, in terms of both perceived social hierarchies and the World War Two militarisation of the population. So, among the membership we had an Air Vice-Marshall, a Brigadier General, a Brigadier, Commanders, Captains, a Lieutenant Colonel, a Major, an OBE, an MBE, a knight, a JP, and several doctors. There was even an MP on the waiting list. All other members are referred to as Mr or with the suffix of Esquire but, tellingly, the bailiff is addressed merely by his surname!

Dr Harry Orr and Commander Walter Smith RN would become very long-standing custodians of the Tonford Fly Fishing Club. Harry Orr was the Chairman from 1951 to 1994 and probably the most significant individual in the club's history.

Dr Henry Richardson Orr CBE was born in Cardiff in 1912 to Scottish parents. His father was a university lecturer. By 1939, Harry was a biology lecturer at Derby Technical College. His first wife Lily died at the age of 36 in 1948. During the war they had both been civilian voluntary first-aiders.

In 1945, Orr was appointed both Headmaster of the Canterbury Technical High School for Boys (later re-named Geoffrey Chaucer Technical School, Geoffrey Chaucer School, Chaucer Technology School and sometimes it was simply known as 'Chaucer'). He was also Principal of the Canterbury Evening Institute. Under Harry Orr the evening institute developed into Canterbury Technical College, which, in turn, would become today's Canterbury College. Both institutions shared the same site.

Dr Henry Richardson Orr CBE 1912-2004.

With the growth of the Technical Institute, Orr's assistant was appointed 'Master in Charge' of the High School while Orr remained as Principal of the Technical Institute. He seems to have been unhappy about this. His unexpected resignation in 1955 caused plans for the major redevelopment of the College buildings to be abandoned for two years. After leaving Canterbury Institute, he became Principal of Medway and Maidstone College of Technology (now MidKent College) for many years. He was awarded the CBE for Services to Education in the 1970 New Year's Honours list while in that post. He married his second wife, Phyllis, in 1978, when he was 66 years of age. Tim Greenfield, the proprietor of a local shooting ground, lodge, and field sports shop, who was club secretary for 13 years, described Harry to me as 'like a country GP, a really nice man and an excellent fly tyer.'

Harry Orr announced that he had 'hung up his rods' at the 1995 AGM when he was presented with an engraved memento and was 'unreservedly and unanimously' granted Honorary Life Membership 'with deep gratitude for all that he had done to make the club such a success.' He fished on, occasionally, until at least 2000. He died aged 92 in 2004.

Commander Walter Smith RN, who would become a member of the CDAA Committee in the early 1970s, was TFFC Secretary from 1951 to 1965. Later, when his eyesight started to fail, he was unable to continue as TFFC Secretary but nevertheless wanted to continue to serve the club. He therefore served as Treasurer from 1965 to 1974.

The handling of Walter Smith's departure from the club seems to have been rather unfortunate. When other long serving club officers retired this was generally noted at the AGM with a presentation of some sort. Smith seems to have 'slipped quietly out of the back door.' In poor health, in December 1974 he wrote a short and rather sad letter to the club resigning his membership adding 'Goodbye to all. It has been nice to know you,' and, regrettably, that was that. It is incredibly sad that a man who was undoubtedly a great servant of the club was allowed to leave in this way.

On 20 April 1951, before the first TFFS Annual General Meeting, the founding Sub-Committee met with AVM Fraser who agreed that in anticipation of the new lease, he would allow fishing to start on 1st of May 1951. The Tonford Fly Fishing Section's very first action was therefore to order 250 twelve-inch brown trout from Weston Fishery and after a short delay these were stocked on 12th of May.

The CDAA sent invitations to join the Tonford Fly Fishing Section to all its 467 members and by the end of April 1951 thirteen members had applied; and, while the Sub-Committee was authorised to advertise for members, it wasn't necessary as by October there was already a waiting list. The first AGM took place on Friday 25th May in the library of Canterbury Technical Institute where Dr Orr was Principal. By that date, seventeen members had been elected and nine of them were present. Dr Orr was formally elected Chairman, and Commander Smith was elected Secretary. Dr McNaught and Mr Mostyn Scott were elected to the Sub-Committee and Mr Cooke was nominated by the CDAA. At that meeting, as it would be at such meetings over the next 70 years, concern was expressed about the bailiff's power to control poaching, and members were urged to join weed-cutting parties!

Other perennial problems were soon to raise their heads. The Sub-Committee became concerned about nuisance from boats on the water, especially at weekends. An examination of the legal title suggested that the boats were trespassing, but it was resolved that before any offender would be challenged the club should take legal advice. To incur this expenditure, they would need the authority of the CDAA Management Committee – one of the disadvantages of being a mere 'Section.' However, the Tonford Committee (it now described itself as a Committee rather than a Sub-Committee) decided that whatever the legal position, the Section's policy would always be to offer boaters and canoeists 'a friendly compromise, without prejudice.' Nevertheless, the Chairman would soon report that he had turned two canoes off the river! Bathers and trespassers were also a continuing problem, and it was agreed to erect notice boards to support members in their 'good tempered efforts to discourage offenders while maintaining the goodwill of the non-fishing public.' Seventy years later, this remains the policy of the club.

In November 1951, the Committee considered the draft lease, and this was passed to the CDAA for approval. By March 1952, amendments put forward by the CDAA and Air Vice-Marshall Fraser had been agreed and the Section had good reason to believe that the Section and its fishing had been secured for the foreseeable future. However, a critical juncture in the history of the Club was looming.

Air Vice-Marshall Hugh Henry Macleod Fraser, Companion of the Order of the Bath, was a wealthy and well-connected man with a military bearing and background. He was apparently somewhat difficult and could be unreasonable and short-tempered. He was always eager to gain the maximum income from his fishing property. Indeed, Walter Smith described him as 'grasping.'

Fraser expected and was given the deference that the societal norms of post-war Britain demanded. This deference extended to doing whatever was required to avoid upsetting him and thereby risking the renewal of the lease. This included: allowing Fraser and his guests to fish the Club water; inviting Fraser and his wife to the Annual Dinner; sending him an annual report, and informally agreeing to stock his private fishing above Milton Bridge at the Section's expense.

Nevertheless, it is recorded that Fraser later reduced the rent from £120 pa to £60 pa, albeit on the understanding that the Section would spend the difference on river maintenance and improvements.

In February 1954, with the renewal of the lease on the horizon, the Committee considered a letter from Air Vice-Marshall Fraser in which he sought its reaction to an increase in rent from £60 to £90 pa, with the Section to pay any increase in the local authority rates. The Committee accepted the rent increase but was worried about taking on the rates as a rating re-assessment was imminent and it was estimated that the current liability of £1.2s.4d to the Bridge Blean Rural District Council might well rise to £50 or £100. Critically, in this letter to Orr, AVM Fraser used the title *Tonford Fly Fishing Association*. This suggested that he envisaged that the Tonford Section might break away from the CDAA and seek its own lease of the water. The embarrassed Committee resolved to make it clear to the CDAA that it was not seeking a breakaway.

A dispute with one of the Section's neighbours would eventually precipitate the breakaway from the CDAA. In June 1954 it was reported to the Committee that Mr Griffiths, the new owner of Little Cottage, Ashford Road, had cut a launching slip and had put a boat on the river and was fishing from it, despite being advised by the CDAA bailiff and a member, Mr Little, that it was not allowed. Fraser visited Griffiths and made the legal position clear, but in pursuit of friendly relations with Thannington residents he told Griffiths that he could keep his boat and fishing, subject to certain restrictions. The Tonford Committee was very unhappy with this and drafted a letter to Fraser advising against granting

Griffiths any special privileges, as other residents had removed their boats when requested and it would create a dangerous precedent.

Fraser took great exception to the Tonford Committee's advice. Without even reading the whole of their letter, he lost his temper and wrote a response, for which he later expressed regret, in which he questioned whether the Section was a suitable tenant of his water. He ordered the Section to permit Griffiths to fish from his garden on two days a week. Of course, he had no legal right to order any such thing. Fraser then inexplicably offered to compensate Griffiths to the tune of £70. Griffiths accepted and, ill-advisedly, Fraser paid up. The Committee did not approve of Fraser's settlement with Griffiths which went totally contrary to the legal realities. Nevertheless, they needed to appease Fraser as the lease would soon be expiring, so they offered Fraser £25 towards his expenses. He accepted the £25, which Dr Orr paid, but stated that he thought that the CDAA should also contribute. He claimed that by not responding quickly enough to a letter to them from Griffiths the CDAA had caused the delay during which Griffiths had incurred expenditure (presumably for the construction of the slipway and the purchase of the boat). Despite this compensation, Griffiths was still fishing illegally five years later and was still being told that he should not!

Over the summer, Fraser wrote to Dr Orr stating that he preferred to deal with 'Dr Orr and his friends' rather than the CDAA. He offered a lease at £50 per year 'plus a gentleman's agreement on other points.' After his impetuous reaction to the Section's letter, he may have been trying to redeem himself. The Section's ordinary members were simply informed that a disagreement had arisen between Air Vice-Marshall Fraser and the CDAA and that the Committee would be drafting a constitution and revised rules for a new association to be inaugurated at the next General Meeting. Thus, Fraser's hasty and volatile nature gave rise to the independent Tonford Fly Fishing Club.

Formation of The Tonford Fly Fishing Club

The Committee instructed solicitors to draft a lease and submit it to Fraser's lawyers. This was for a seven-year term at a rent of £70 pa. The new association agreed to pay the rates to Blean Bridge RDC, for the Chairman had been told that the rate reassessment was likely to be between £5 and £10 and not the £50 to £100 that had been feared. Fraser did not want a third party to think that the CDAA was in any way involved, so the title 'Section' could no longer be used. The Committee proposed that the new title should be 'The Tonford Fly Fishing Association.' It hoped to maintain friendly relationship with the CDAA, and it was subsequently agreed that new members would be recruited only from the membership of the CDAA. The continuing close relationship between the two associations was evident when the TFFC subsequently loaned the CDAA £100 to assist with legal costs in a pollution case against South Eastern Tar Distillers, and in their invitations to the CDAA President and his wife to attend TFFC Annual Dinners.

With the Tonford Section taking over its own financial responsibilities, Commander Alexander Blackley Goble RN was temporarily appointed as Treasurer. After a long and distinguished career in the Royal Navy, Goble served with the

Royal National Lifeboat Institution for many years and was awarded its silver medal for risking his life to save others.

Cmdr. Alexander Blackley-Goble RN 1898-1967

Despite the 'temporary' nature of his initial appointment, Goble, who was from an aristocratic family, would serve the Club for many years as Treasurer and later as Secretary.

An Extraordinary General Meeting of the CDAA Tonford Fly Fishing Section was held on 15th December 1954 in the library of Canterbury Technical Institute. It was formally decided that the **Tonford Fly Fishing Club** should be formed from all existing members of the Section and that this would take over the Tonford fishery at the expiry of the current lease on 31st March 1955

It was agreed that Air Vice-Marshall Fraser should be deemed a member and be allowed to fish the water with two guests. Perhaps, along with the stocking of his private beat, this was one of the 'private arrangements' that he had earlier alluded to. Fraser suggested that he should approve the Rules and Byelaws of the new Club, but in a surprising demonstration of newfound independence, the Club rejected his suggestion, asserting that the membership alone should govern members' behaviour.

After this inaugural meeting, the Committee decided to invite Air Vice-Marshall Fraser to serve as Club President, which he accepted. He remained in this office until his death in January 1962 at the age of 66 years. He had long suffered from hypertension. The Club recorded its sadness at his passing.

Tonford Fly Fishing Club has always warmly acknowledged its descent from The Canterbury and District Angling Association.

The original Club Rules and Byelaws are reproduced in an appendix.

Thus, the **Tonford Fly Fishing Club** was established on the 15th of December 1954.

Chapter Two

The Evolution of the Fishery

The River Stour

The Upper Great Stour first emanates from springs in the clay substrata in the Lenham area before running eastwards where it is soon joined by the East Stour near Ashford. As the River Great Stour, it then flows past Wye and Chilham to Chartham where today the Club's water begins at Chartham Corn Mill. From there, the Club's waters stretch to just outside Canterbury. The river then flows through the City to Sandwich and the Stour Marshes to reach the sea via Pegwell Bay.

Below Wye, the Great Stour becomes a chalkstream. These are rivers whose water mainly arises from springs in a chalk substratum. Rainwater falling on the hills is filtered by the chalk before emerging from springs rich in minerals but low in particulates. Chalkstream water is alkaline and crystal clear and generally about 10'C throughout the year. Chalkstreams are prized by anglers because they provide an ideal habitat for trout and salmon. They are, however, a scarce and vulnerable resource. Bernard Venables, the celebrated angling author and artist, who once fished the Tonford waters, described the chalkstreams as 'rivers of idealised imagining...so improbably pure, so crystalline, so opulently stocked with great trout.'

While a classic chalkstream enjoys a fairly constant water flow, the Great Stour can flood in winter and run very low in summer because in addition to spring water, it receives rainwater runoff from agricultural land and is subject to licensed abstraction. Rainwater can put the river into spate and colour the water and bring pollution from agricultural chemicals and animal waste. The river also receives the recycled outfall from several wastewater treatment works, notably at Ashford, Wye, Chilham and Chartham, and treated effluent from the Chartham Paper Mill. The Mill does not abstract water from the river, but from its own borehole. In dry weather a significant proportion of the river flow is made up of licensed discharges of treated effluent. In times of flood, the amount of water reaching wastewater treatment works can exceed its recycling capacity and, despite many control measures, polluting water may legally be discharged into the river. There may well also be unlicensed discharges. The river water quality can also be affected by road run-off, storm overflows, and localised flooding such as when sewage pumps fail, or sewers become blocked.

Along the Stour Valley, licensed ground water abstraction at Godmersham, Chilham, Howfield and Thannington, can reduce the flow and thereby increase the deposition of silt and the concentration of pollutants. This has been an issue of great concern to the Club over the years. Nitrates and phosphates from agricultural run-off and wastewater outfalls probably account for the prolific weed growth from which the river suffers in the summer.

The Club's Fishery Over the Years

The length of the Great Stour leased by the Club in 1951 from Air Vice-Marshal Fraser today comprises the Club's Upper, Middle and Lower Tonford beats. Fraser also had rights above the Bridge, then known colloquially as the 'Top Water', but he retained this length for his personal use. The Club's original length extended from the Milton road-bridge down to the western boundary of the City of Canterbury 'to the carrier entering the river on the Northwest bank next above the first viaduct'. In Club papers, it is described as 'one mile and two furlongs' or '2000 yards' long. This was a relatively short length for a club of 25 members of which eight rods were allowed to fish at any one time (though not within 100yds of each other). Indeed, in the early years there were proposals to reduce the number of members, but this was overruled by the financial implications.

The Upper Tonford Beat in 1930

In the early 1950s, barbed wire along the river made it difficult for members to reach the water, and it could limit back casts. It was discovered that it contravened the owner's legal title – but the TFFS decided to seek 'friendly compromises' where possible. It nevertheless wanted to determine the extent of its rights, and instructed Kingsfords Solicitors in Canterbury for advice. It also contacted the Anglers Cooperative Association. Later, legal advice was given pro bono by Mr Allbutt, a Canterbury solicitor and kindly member. If legal action were to be taken, the Committee felt that they would need the security of a long lease, and so at an early stage they sought an amendment to extend the draft lease to five years with an option for a further five years.

Even a lease of five years introduced uncertainty and anxiety, particularly when renewal time approached. It was therefore prudent to constantly defer to AVM Fraser. Plans for the 1954 Annual Dinner were cancelled because the Committee felt that it would be too anxious about the future of the Club to enjoy it, and speeches about the future of the lease would be uncomfortable in the presence of Fraser, who, as President, had to be invited and feted. Fortunately, a new lease was agreed with him and signed in January 1955.

While the river was the main focus of the Club's attention, when the Committee was notified in April 1958 that the Brett Group, the local aggregate firm, had bought the land on the North bank below Tonford Bridge, they resolved to seek the fishing rights of the gravel pits that would be excavated there. This plan never materialised.

The Club also heard that Bretts had acquired Milton Manor and that Mr W. Brett would live there. It was said that Brett intended to keep the South bank fishing of the 'Top Water' for his own use. AVM Fraser had the lease on the fishing from the opposite bank and the Club had felt obliged to stock this length for him. In January 1959 Fraser wrote to the Club saying that he had agreed with Mr Brett that in future they would both stock the Top Water, and he expected the Club to continue to do this on his behalf! He also said that he intended to increase the Tonford rent to £100pa. Fraser was entitled to give notice in September that he would terminate the lease agreement, so, as usual, the Club was fearful of upsetting him, but they resolved to get some assurance from him of the first option to renew the lease or to purchase the rights from him or his estate in the case of his demise, for the Committee was aware that Fraser had been suffering ill health for some time. Fraser agreed, but he resisted putting it in writing.

The new 10-year lease, with the proviso that either party could terminate after 5 years, was indeed signed by AVM and Mrs Fraser but not in their personal capacities. They signed in the name of a private company that they had formed with their daughter: 'Property Management (Southern) Ltd'. The original lease with Fraser had provided him with membership of the Club and the right to bring two guests onto Club water. The Committee had intended this benefit for AVM Fraser personally, but now that the lease was in the name of a company it wasn't clear who would enjoy the benefit. The Committee expressed concern that 'it might be used by the office boy!'

On 18th January 1962, Air Vice-Marshal Hugh Henry Macleod Fraser CB passed away at his home in Twyford, Hampshire. The Committee sent its condolences to Mrs Hester Fraser and a donation to the RAF Benevolent Fund. Members stood in silence at the AGM in respect for his memory.

Fraser's death introduced yet more anxiety about the future of the fishing and the Club. The Club had a lease to 31st March 1970 but there was the option for Fraser's company to break out on 31st March 1965. The Committee was concerned that other individuals and clubs might approach the company with an offer to purchase. The Club therefore resolved to approach the company to affirm that it wished to purchase. Meanwhile, the Club Rules were amended to allow Mrs Fraser and two guests to fish Club water. She was also invited to attend the AGM and to succeed her husband as Club President. While Mrs Fraser firmly declined the invitation to become President, the Club was relieved to hear that she had no intention to sell and that if she did sell, the club would be given the first option to buy the rights. Nevertheless, the Club started to consider its position should it lose its water. It even took legal advice on how its funds should be disposed of in the event of the Club disbanding.

In March, the Club's Chairman, Dr Harry Orr, told the Committee that he had been in private correspondence with Mrs Fraser and there was a possibility that she might lease the Top Water (today known as the Milton beat) to the Club. The Committee was attracted by the idea of adding the Top Water to its fishery and it authorised Dr Orr to meet with Mrs Fraser and to negotiate a lease at up to £75 pa. Later in the year it was discovered that the Stour Fishery Association, a much wealthier entity than the TFFC, had also approached Mrs Fraser about taking the lease. You might imagine that there were some raised eyebrows, if not hackles, when Orr subsequently reported to the Committee that he had met with Mrs Fraser and he had taken the lease on the Top Water for himself, and not for the Club!

Concerns about the future of the fishing and the Club forced the Committee to look for other water. They considered the Ickham Flyfishers length of the Lesser Stour, which was partly owned by members of that club and partly by the Church Commissioners, but that lease would not be available until 1967. The Secretary had heard that the Stour Fishery

Association would not be renewing its lease on a stretch of the Great Stour at Godmersham, where, apparently, the owner 'didn't like them'. It was decided to follow this up and eventually the water was formally offered to the Club by the owner. Surprisingly, the offer was then declined as the Committee believed that 'it was not good fishing'.

The lease on the Tonford fishing next fell due in 1970 and after difficult negotiations it was renewed for five years. The signing of a further new lease was announced at the 1975 AGM in the presence of Mrs Hester Fraser who had at last agreed to become Club President 'to the acclamation of members present'. Fishing was therefore assured to 1980, when again the lease was extended.

Unfortunately, Mrs Fraser suffered a severe stroke in 1982 and in her place the Club had to deal with her daughter, Miss Elizabeth Fraser. The 1983 AGM was informed of the death of Mrs Hester Fraser, the Club President, and members stood in silence to express their respect.

Anxiety levels were raised once again in the period coming up to the 1985 lease renewal. Miss Elizabeth Fraser had indicated that she might sell and had instructed professional valuers. They advised her that a reasonable rent for the Tonford water would be £2,500 pa whereas the Club had been paying £1,000 pa. Fearful of losing its water, the Committee had little choice but to make a better offer. Its bid of £2100 pa for the first three years of the term with a rent review after that, was accepted, but, worryingly, by the start of the 1985 season the Club had not received the lease for signature. Without a lease they felt unable to pay the rent. In anticipation of matters being soon settled, the Committee delayed stocking but told members to fish as usual. Miss Fraser was apparently waiting for a Court decision on the interpretation of *The Landlord and Tenant Act* that might affect the Club's position before she would sign the lease, but that didn't stop her charging the Club £150 interest for late payment plus £350 for her legal fees. Being anxious to avoid conflict with its landlord, the Club reluctantly agreed to pay. By the start of fishing in 1986, the Club still did not have a lease. Members fished on. One of the Club officers wrote that 'Miss Fraser is twice as difficult to deal with as her mother, if that were possible'.

In 1988 Miss Fraser announced her intention to sell the fishing rights for £150,000. The Club considered how the money might be raised. But by 1989 her asking price had increased to £350,000, a sum that was way beyond what the Club could afford. The Club sought legal opinion on its rights should the title pass to a third party. An Extraordinary General Meeting was called in October when members were told that Miss Fraser had negotiated a sale to the Brett Group for £300,000. Club members authorised the Committee to negotiate a lease with Bretts up to the surprising maximum of £7,000 p.a. Club Treasurer Mr Richard Tuttle, a land agent, led the negotiations, but Bretts later withdrew from the sale and the fishing remained unsold. Eventually, in 1991, a new lease was granted to the Club. The Milton to Horton 'Top Water' passed from Dr Orr to the Club at some time during this period and it may have been included in this lease.

In 1991, Bretts granted the lease of the South bank of the 'Top Water', opposite the Club's length, to the Stour Fishery Association. This was in return for allowing Bretts to put a bridge over the SFA's own water. The Club was unaware of this until it was a 'fait accompli'. Members were concerned about the stocking implications and also because fly fishing from the South bank is very difficult for most of its length, and both SFA and TFFC members would have the right to wade to the middle of the stream. The SFA subsequently approached the Club for permission to fish from the North side. They were refused, but an agreement was later reached to share the cost of stocking the Top Water. The Club always endeavoured to keep on good terms with the SFA. The SFA have always supported our Club.

With continuing uncertainty about the future of the Tonford lease, in 1995 the Club considered once again whether to try to purchase rather than lease the water. Purchase would cost an average of £2000 per member, and there was also concern that the growth and development of Ashford might jeopardise the future of the river and its value in the long term, but the club nevertheless decided to continue to investigate the purchase option.

In 1999, Miss Fraser very firmly stated that the club's lease would not be renewed after 1999 and that she intended to sell the fishing rights of the Tonford stretch. The asking price was now £200,000, a figure that was well beyond the Club's reach. Dr Jack Cohen, the Secretary at that time, entered into purchase negotiations with her on behalf of the Club and instructed an independent appraisal of the river. The Club's consultant found various problems and areas for improvement and therefore valued the fishing rights at just £50,000, a figure that Miss Fraser was unlikely to even consider. The Club being eager to retain its water was nevertheless prepared to go to £100,000. It was planned to raise the money by selling shares in a private company established for the purpose. However, in August 1999 the Club heard that the rights had been sold over its head to Mid Kent Water for £180,000. This could have been the death knell of the Tonford Fly Fishing Club, but under Chairman Mr Michael Ross Browne, Secretary Dr Jack Cohen, and Treasurer Mr John Dawson, an architect, the Club held together and started to look for new water.

The Mid Kent Fisheries Syndicate

The new owners, Mid Kent Water (nowadays incorporated into South East Water), announced that the Tonford fishery would in future be managed by Mid Kent Fisheries (MKF), on a syndicate basis. MKF invited TFFC officers to a meeting in December when they explained that they would not lease to the Club but instead would offer syndicate memberships to those Club members that applied before the end of February. This undermined the very existence of the Club. MKF's annual fee would be £300 (later they increased this to £375) compared with the £175 that TFFC had charged. MKF's justification for the increase being that members would be able to fish not only the Tonford water but also a length of the river at Chilham Mill. Also, many tasks previously undertaken by Club members on a voluntary basis, such as administration, stocking, weed cutting, etc, would in future be provided on a commercial basis, and of course VAT had to be paid. MKF outlined its plans for the syndicate and fishery:

- the syndicate would be run as a new club, with an AGM, etc;
- the maximum membership fishing the Tonford and Chilham beats would be 40;

- a bridge would be built from the car park field to the north bank (it later became apparent that this was intended for the benefit of anglers fishing MKF's lake on that side);
- a fence would be erected along the river to prevent sheep eroding the banks, discourage swans from crossing over from the lakes, provide a buffer zone against poachers, dog walkers, etc and to enable beneficial bankside plant life to become re-established;
- the Tonford beat would be stocked at monthly intervals with a total of 500 fish and the Chilham beat with a total of 275 fish;
- the syndicate would be run to TFFC rules except the maximum number of fish killed per session would be reduced to 2 and the TFFC limit of 6 fish per week would no longer apply;
- MKF would provide bailiffs, weed cutting by hand, membership cards, parking disks and all other administrative services, and
- MKF would offer non-members the opportunity to fish as part of a 'hospitality package', and to its guests on 'charity days'. Persons assisting MKF on these charity days would also be allowed to fish, including on the Tonford beat, but this would be on a maximum of 5 days a year.

The Committee was very concerned that after 46 years at Tonford, members were losing control of the fishery and that many would be unable to meet the increased fee. Indeed, the Club might disappear. But, taking a positive perspective, Chairman Michael Ross Browne, wrote to all members advising them of the changes and asking them to give MKF the opportunity 'to demonstrate to all our satisfactions that the improved and extended fishery they envisage genuinely represents good value'. Nevertheless, he added that members' best interests would be served by keeping the Club alive.

Ross Browne's Committee adopted a very clever strategy to preserve the Club, avoid losing members, exert some influence over the future of the fishery, and safeguard Club members' value for money. Rather than leaving members to deal directly with MKF, as MKF had wanted, he asked them to send their usual annual subscription cheque for £175 to the Club to which the Club would add a subsidy of £200 before submitting syndicate subscriptions en-masse to MKF in two instalments. At a swiftly arranged AGM, all members present agreed to this approach. Thirty-two of the questionnaires sent to the Club's 33 members were returned, and all indicated a willingness to fish in 2000 under Ross Browne's proposals. The Club passed £13,375 to Mid Kent Fisheries on its members' behalf in this way and looked forward optimistically to the new arrangements. Unfortunately, things did not go well.

Before the next AGM the Chairman wrote to members stating that he knew that many of them were dissatisfied with the way the fishery had been managed over this first year. Both he and the Secretary had been so dismayed by MKF's attitude and performance that they had been trying for months to find an alternative stretch of the Great Stour for the Club. They were hopeful, but it was unlikely to be arranged before the start of the season. One member summed it up when he wrote in response:

> 'I would give anything to maintain our fishing club as it was. It was a sad day when MKF took over the Tonford beat. I do not like their attitude and I will not continue my MKF membership next season. I fully support the efforts of the Committee and would dearly like to see the continuation of TFFC fishing the River Stour and returning to the happy times that we once enjoyed.'

Despite the promised stocking, members with many years' experience of the Tonford water reported little, if any, contact with stocked fish. Indeed, members reported that there was little evidence of any fish at all! The Club wrote to MKF for information on catch returns but it received no response, despite reminders. That was why the Kendrick Cup (see Chapter 4) was not awarded that year. A straw poll at the 2001 TFFC AGM suggested that over the season those members present had caught sixty-four trout, which extrapolated to 120 for the whole membership. The previous year they had caught 339. Further, visitors had been sold day tickets, the MKF syndicate membership was not forty as envisaged but 55, and a maximum of 3 days fishing per week rule had been introduced unilaterally. The promised Syndicate AGM had not taken place, and TFFC's request for a meeting with MKF had been rebuffed. While syndicate rules limited members to two fish a day, it was claimed that one MKF guest at Chilham had been allowed to kill fourteen fish on one day (it was suggested that Chilham was 'mini-stocked' before visits by guests). It seemed that every promise made by MKF at the outset had been broken.

Members expressed their total dissatisfaction with the management of the water by MKF. Since MKF's response to earlier communications had been negative or non-existent, it was unanimously agreed that the Chairman should send a letter to the Managing Director of Mid Kent Water which would include a statement that many TFFC members would not be renewing their syndicate memberships until things were put right. Clearly, members were most unhappy with Mid Kent Fisheries at that time. The Minutes record that eventually by 2008 good relations with MKF had been restored.

The Club decided not to subsidise syndicate membership in 2001. With no Club water, it was decided that no TFFC membership subscription would be payable that year. This could have been the end of the Club.

New Club Waters

Members stayed loyal. They voted not to disband the Club and that Club funds should be retained pending the acquisition of new water.

In 2002, Michael Ross Browne and Jack Cohen concluded negotiations with Peter Bracher of the Stour Fishery Association for the Horton beat. This beat ran from the confluence at Chartham village to the wooden footbridge at the Horton sewage works. Neil Jones, then a TFFC Committee member and later Club Secretary, reported that it was very amicable, a 'gentleman's agreement, sealed at The Woolpack in Chilham'. Seventeen members had stayed with the Club, and membership was limited to just 20 to avoid overcrowding the new beat. Even with just 20, the Club had to introduce a rota system that allocated priority to four named members each day.

Chartham Corn Mill 1930

In 2004, the 'Deanery' beat, from Chartham Corn Mill weir to the railway bridge was added with no extra rent being demanded by our landlord, the Stour Fishery Association, which was, as ever, supportive of our Club.

Sadly, in 2007, Chairman Mr Michael Ross Browne of Petham, passed away at the early age of 59 after a short illness.

Mr Michael Ross Browne 1948-2007

Michael Ross Browne, a Cambridge graduate, and a specialist in pisciculture, was the proprietor of a Whitstable seafood business. He was a descendant of the Browne family that in medieval times held both Tonford and Milton manors. He led the Club superbly and successfully through these difficult times. A former Secretary described him to me as 'a real gentleman in every sense of the word.' Several members attended his funeral, and at the Club's AGM members stood in silence to show their respect. It was agreed to make a substantial donation to charity in his memory. Dr Jack Cohen, from Birchington, took over as Chairman and Neil Jones was elected Secretary in Jack's place.

Dr Jack Bernard Cohen 1946 -2021

Dr Jack Bernard Cohen passed away during the writing of this book. He was well-known and respected both as a dentist and as a local politician, having served on Lewisham, Thanet, and

Dover Councils, and as Chairman of Nonington and Birchington Parish Councils. He was an examiner with the Royal College of Surgeons and a clinical tutor at King's College London. Jack reached the rank of Major in the army and later was commissioned in the Territorials, being mobilised during the first Gulf War.

In 2007 the Milton beat, the South bank of the old 'Top Water', from Bretts wooden footbridge at Horton to the Milton road-bridge, was sold, and in 2010 the Committee was able to negotiate a lease from the new owners, our good friends the Stour Fishery Association.

The two pools below the railway bridge at the bottom of the Deanery beat were added in 2009 and the short Paper Mill beat was added in 2010. This gave the Club the entire fishable stretch of the Great Stour (outside the Paper Mill) from Chartham Corn Mill to the Milton Bridge. These additions enabled the membership to be increased to 25 and later to 30.

The Return to Tonford

The Tonford beat remained with Mid Kent Fisheries until it was offered for sale in 2011. The Stour Fishery Association tried to acquire the rights, but it was apparently outbid by London financier and keen fly fisher, Mr Mark Evans. Mr Evans described to me how he had first tried fly fishing in 2003 and was immediately hooked. He resolved to acquire some fishing rights, and, by chance, the Tonford water became available at that time. He told me 'Good fishing rarely comes on the market. This was a substantial length of water and close to home. It seemed good value and so I decided to go for it!'

Mr Mark Evans fishing at Tonford

At Tonford Mr Evans owns not just the fishing rights but the land under the river with the right of access to the water over adjoining land.

Fortunately, TFFC Chairman Jack Cohen found Mr Evans to be 'helpful and approachable' and he was able to negotiate a lease in time for the 2012 season. Thus, after a break of 10 years the Club was able to return to its much-loved Tonford beat and now was able to offer fishing on the Great Stour from Chartham Corn Mill down to the outskirts of the City of Canterbury. Jack Cohen told the 2012 AGM that 'Mr Mark Evans could not have been more helpful. Re-establishing the TFFC on the Tonford beat could not have gone smoother'. The membership was overjoyed to return to its home beat.

Mid Kent Fisheries retained the Chilham beat for trout fishing but otherwise concentrated on coarse fishing in the lakes around Chilham and Chartham, which include some of the best carp fishing in the UK. There is some irony in that former syndicate members were advised by MKF to join the TFFC if they wished to continue to fish the Tonford beats.

The following summarises the evolution of the lengths of the Great Stour fished by TFFC members.

Tonford   1951 - 2000, 2001* and 2011 - present

Chilham   2001*

Horton   2002 - present

Deanery   2004 - present

Paper Mill   2010 – present

Milton   2012 - present

*Mid Kent Fisheries syndicate water fished by TFFC members

Chapter Three

The Club's Waters

The Great Stour Way

The most profound and lasting change to the Club's fishery over the last 70 years came with the opening of the Great Stour Way in 2011. This was first mooted in 1993. It is a hard surfaced path, part of the National Cycle Network, which runs alongside the river from Canterbury to Chartham. While it is undeniably a great asset for walkers and cyclists, it has changed the character of the fishery's environment and has brought many challenges to the Club's fishing. It has also much reduced its value. When the Club's first lease on the Tonford water was signed there was no public right of way along the riverbank below Milton Bridge. Now, while the public merely has a right of way over the path, the river is partly unfenced and this invites public access to the water all along the Club's Tonford, Milton and Horton beats.

Along with Mid Kent Fisheries, the Stour Fisheries Association, riparian and other landowners, the Club was consulted at the planning stage of the 'cycle path' by the Canterbury City Council. At the time, the Club held just the Deanery and Horton beats. In April 2009, the Club submitted its written objections in very strong terms. Chairman Dr Jack Cohen drew attention to the particular risk to fast moving unseen cyclists from back casts. He made 'the most serious objections' on the grounds of public safety, danger to wildlife and, prophetically, the promotion of anti-social and criminal behaviour along the river. Drawing upon Izaak Walton's respect for the Great Stour's sea trout, Cohen highlighted the threats of pollution, vandalism, and poaching. He stressed the Club's long tradition of caring for the river and its vital role in conservation. He asked not for the project to be abandoned but for changes to its form and proximity to the river. In addition, some Club members submitted their individual objections. Club Secretary Mr Anthony Pound attended the Council's Development Control Committee Meeting and gave a verbal submission.

Anthony Pound, of Marshborough, is a designer and a specialist in the conservation and restoration of old buildings. He was introduced to the club by Mr Michael Ross Browne and very soon after that he accepted the role of Club Secretary, a post he held for over ten years. For four of those years he fulfilled the onerous duties of both secretary and treasurer.

Mr Pound described the Council's decision on the night as a 'fait accompli'. Only the slightest precis of the Club's arguments was presented to the elected members in the report by the Council officers to the Council's Development Committee, and, in the face of support from the Environment Agency, the NHS, the Ramblers Association, the Kent Wildlife Trust, and Natural England, the project was approved. On the issue of conflict between the new users and fly fishermen, the Council responded that 'it would be incumbent on all those using the route *and taking advantage of the leisure opportunities offered by the river,* to respect others' right to be present'. It is important to note that no-one has a right to use the river here other than the riparian owner and his lessee, the Club. A Council officer assured me that the objective was merely a path to take cyclists and walkers safely off the A28. In my view, it should have foreseen that in the minds of the public it was opening the river as a general leisure facility. The rights of the riparian owner seem to have been neglected.

By 2012, within a year of the new cycle route's opening, houseowners on the Tonford stretch were already complaining of 'constant anti-social behaviour by persons walking the path' and unauthorised persons entering the river.

While it was promoted by Kent Highways as a cycling route, today there are more walkers than cyclists and the route also provides access for canoeists, poachers, and sometimes unruly youths. Fly fishers seeking the isolation and tranquillity of the river may sometimes have to contend with: swimmers and sunbathers; dogs fetching sticks from the water; barbecues; campers; litter; canoes; paddleboards, and inflatables. Occasionally there are difficult confrontations with boaters and with poachers. The problems are exacerbated at weekends and in school holidays and good weather. Fortunately, most fishing takes place in the early morning and the evening.

In May 2020 during the pandemic lockdown, there was a period of record sunshine and high temperatures. Solitary fishing was allowed, but despite government exhortations 'to stay at home' and to 'keep social distance', there could be so many members of the non-fishing public using some stretches of the river that flyfishing became impossible during what is traditionally the most enjoyable and productive time of the year for Club members – the Mayfly season.

At the end of this chapter a table shows the different beat descriptors used by the Club over the years.

The Upper Deanery Beat

The Deanery beat takes its name from Deanery Farm through which it passes. 'Deanery House' is a Grade 2* listed building that dates from the early 14th century, with later Jacobean additions and features. Some of the farm buildings are also listed. The Deanery was originally the country house of the Priors of Christ Church Canterbury. After the reformation it was used by the Deans of Canterbury, hence the name.

Chartham Corn Mill, Weir, and Mill Pool

The fishing beat starts at Chartham Corn Mill. This is a mid-19th century complex of buildings, listed Grade 2, on the site of a previous mill that was destroyed in a fire. All the buildings have now been converted to residential use. The mill race does not appear to flow, but the main river discharges powerfully into the mill pool over a weir, bringing food for the resident fish and oxygenating the water. The pool is known to hold a few sea trout and perhaps it sometimes even holds a few salmon. It can be productive for brown trout throughout the season to both upstream dry flies and nymphs. The Environment Agency recently installed a fish ladder in its attempts to preserve and improve the sea trout run here.

During the summer school holidays the pool often attracts local teenagers who gather and swim in the pool, despite it being private and the danger from underwater hazards including the remains of a revetment on the South side.

During the 2020 pandemic lockdown the pool became an immensely popular daytime attraction and fishing there became impossible.

The pool with its fast water is also attractive to canoeists, despite the 'No Boating and Canoeing' signs.

Below the pool is a delightful chalkstream length with gravel bed, several riffles, and overhanging trees. A 2010 study by the Wild Trout Trust found this length to be the only spawning habitat on the Club's water upstream of Chartham Village.

The dilapidated bridge here was originally constructed by the Bretts Group when they operated a quarry on the South side. The Company received the Quarry Products Association Award for its sympathetic restoration of the former quarry back to grazing land.

Looking Downstream from the Deanery Mill Pool

The Lower Deanery Beat

This beat runs from the confluence of the main river, the mill race and a narrow drain (the weir on the mill race at this point is nowadays barely visible) to the trees on the South bank about 100 yards below the Parish Road bridge.

The Lower Deanery, looking upstream

The water below Brett's Bridge is popular with members for its secluded rural nature, but it is too slow and deep and silted for a true chalkstream trout habitat. This results from past dredging, bank alterations, and the flow being controlled by a weir downstream at Chartham Paper Mill. The Club has on several occasions lobbied for the water level to be lowered, but Mr Mark Hobday, the manager of the mill, told me that there are major technical constraints in the mill that prevent it. The Wild Trout Trust has recommended that the channel should be radically restricted, and the bed raised with imported gravel. These are expensive solutions, but nevertheless the project remains on the Club's wish list.

The length at 'Riverside' has the road running alongside the North side of the river and, beyond it, a row of houses. When the water was handed over to the Club by the SFA it was pointed out that while some of the Riverside frontagers have boats moored on the river, they have no right to do so, or to navigate the river, or to fish. Nevertheless, at the time of writing, an estate agent is offering a house at Riverside, where the 'residents have adopted the riverbank setting with decking and mooring'. This length of the river is rather prone to weeding up.

Below Riverside the river is crossed by the railway and then the Parish Road Bridge. The length below the Parish Road bridge was formerly known as 'The Paper Mill Beat'. Members rarely fish it, perhaps because some of the residents of the houses opposite have in the past aggressively challenged members' right to be there! The beat finishes at the boundary with the Paper Mill.

Chartham Paper Mill dates from the 18th century. In the 11th century the Domesday Book recorded a corn mill on this site. By the 15th century there was a fulling mill, for cleaning and thickening wool. The paper mill was established in 1730. The mill race here, an artificial channel, dates from the 1830s.

It is recorded that at the time of Edward the First there was a vineyard here. This is notable because Chartham now has a vineyard again, at Burnt House Farm, not far from the river.

The Upper Horton Beat

The Horton beats take their name from the old settlement of Horton (which means muddy village) situated at the boundary between the two Horton beats. The Horton Manor Chapel, currently being restored, sits on the south side of the river at this point. It is a Grade 2 listed building that dates from about 1300. Horton Manor with its two mills was mentioned in the Domesday Book when its Norman new owner was the Bishop of Bayeux, Normandy.

The Upper Horton Beat, Looking Upstream

The Horton Beat runs from the confluence at Chartham Village to the wooden footbridge at the Horton sewage works. The weir at the confluence is on the Chartham Paper Mill race rather than the main river. This weir has recently been fitted with a fish ladder for migratory fish. The deep pool below, at one time known locally as 'Tumbling Bay', is said to hold sea trout in the autumn. It is popular with local swimmers and poachers and is rarely fished by members.

The lakes on the north side of the river at Horton and Milton are the legacy of industrial gravel extraction, now beautifully restored.

Lower Horton Beat

The Lower Horton beat starts at the rickety footbridge and pipe crossing at the Horton settlement. Beyond this is an

Fishing at Lower Horton

environment agency weir and gauging station whose deep pool is another popular location for swimmers and poachers. In the past, salmon were occasionally discovered lying in this area.

The length below the gauging weir is heavily wooded and protected by fencing and brambles. It provides good spawning and nursery habitat. High voltage power cables pass under the river here and are protected with concrete. The banks are faced with concrete in parts on the North side.

On the South bank the trees shield the sewage works behind. An outfall discharges just before the wooden footbridge. The beat ends at the metal footbridge that carries a public footpath over to the old Milton settlement.

The Milton Beat

The name 'Milton' suggests that there was once a mill here, and indeed there were two at the time of the Domesday Book when its Norman new owner was the Archbishop of Canterbury's Sheriff. Milton Manor House on the South side has long since been demolished, but the late 13th century Milton Manor Chapel remains. This was rebuilt in the 1830s and was recently restored by the Brett Group.

The Milton Beat

The Milton beat runs down from the metal footbridge to the Milton road-bridge. This is the old 'Top Water' that was fished on the North side by AVM Fraser, and then leased to the Club's Chairman, Dr Harry Orr. The fishing on the South side of the beat and Lower Horton passed to Mr Brett when he purchased Milton Manor Farm (now the centre of the Brett Group activities) from Mr Tolputt. The South side is now owned by Mr Mark Evans.

When Mr Brett decided to take up fly fishing and make use of his purchase, he found that his casts often ended up in the trees and bushes on the bank opposite. This is, of course,

The Chalkstream Character of the River at Milton

recognised as one of the rites of passage of all fly fishers. Brett asked the Club if the foliage might be cut down. Fearing the loss of this valuable cover for its trout and their spawning redds, the Club responded (perhaps sarcastically) by offering Mr Brett the use of its weir pool at the Milton Bridge for casting practice!

The Milton beat is long and straight and more open than the Horton beats, with trees mainly on the South side. It has a shallow and beautiful chalkstream character with streaming weeds and visible gravel beds and gravel bars.

The Upper Tonford Beat

The Upper Tonford Beat runs from the Milton road-bridge down to the first house on the South bank. There have been many changes to this stretch, even since the Club was formed.

In 1954 a weir was constructed by the Kent River Board about 200 yards below the Milton bridge. The Club raised no objections. It was intended to oxygenate the water and scour the riverbed to provide loose clean gravel for trout redds. Catch returns show that Milton Weir Pool became a productive spot. Unfortunately, by April 1960 it had started to fall into disrepair and the Club had to press the KRB to carry out repairs. Today nothing remains of the weir at Milton apart from some fallen flagstones and a deep pool.

The Club's car park, today rented from the Bretts Group, is a hard standing in the field on the South side, formerly known as 'Tolputts Meadow'. When the Club was formed, there was

The Upper Tonford Beat from the Milton Road-Bridge

a ford opposite the entrance gate but today there is no trace of it other than a stretch of shallow water that members use to wade across the river.

Today it is hard to believe that for several years in the late 1970s and early 1980s gravel extraction operations by the Bretts Group between the river and the railway involved a temporary bridge and conveyor belt over the river to the 'car park field', opposite the entrance gate. The Club was apprehensive of the impact of this bridge on the fish and fishing but was assured by Bretts that a similar bridge over CDAA water had not caused any problems. An exchange of correspondence between the club and Bretts established that any claim by the Club for damages arising from the bridge should be directed to the riparian owner (the Frasers' company) and not to Bretts. When the Club did have cause to complain to Mrs Fraser, she visited the site with Harry Orr and

Richard Tuttle the Club's Treasurer. She was horrified at what she saw and promised to make a lot of fuss with Bretts about it. The outcome is not recorded, but we can assume that she would certainly have made her point! The quarry is now Thannington Lakes, a popular venue for coarse anglers.

In 1994 the Milton Bridge was widened, and a new road and roundabout constructed, for which Mr Brett philanthropically donated the land. When the project was proposed in 1993, the Club raised no objections with the County Council. However, there was a delay in fencing the new road and the open verges tended to invite motorists, canoeists, and poachers to park their cars and walk down to the river. Fortunately, when pressed by the Club, the Council quickly had the fencing work completed.

The bend in the river at the bottom of the car park field is known in the Club as 'Kendrick's Corner' in memory of late member Thomas Kendrick (see Chapter 4).

Above the field on the South side, is a row of trees shielding the Ashford Road. Here until the 18th century was a public execution site known as 'Hanging Bank' that was notorious for the hanging of sheep rustlers. Some members have joked that it should be reinstated, as a warning to canoeists and poachers!

The Middle Tonford Beat

This beat runs down to the Tonford footbridge and the Roman ford that gave its name to Tonford. It is the site of 'The Ford' (1883), the celebrated painting by Thomas Sydney Cooper R.A.

to be found in Canterbury City Art Gallery. I have an original T. S. Cooper on my study wall, inherited from my grandfather, and I must say that I find it dour and most unattractive!

This is also the site of the (allegedly) accidental drowning of Judge Sir James Hales that is said to have been the inspiration for the 'Two Clowns' speech in Shakespeare's Hamlet.

Tonford would gain its second replacement wooden footbridge in 1988 after the bridge was destroyed by the great storm of 1987. The huge timbers that made up the

Club Treasurer Mr Simon Chandler Fishing at Middle Tonford

replacement bridge were ordered from a firm based in Holland. When the articulated lorry bearing the 'bridge kit' arrived, the Dutch driver had great difficulty in getting his vehicle down Tonford Lane. Only after several hours of difficult manoeuvring did he succeed. The timbers were eventually unloaded but were found to be the wrong size and had to be loaded up and sent back to Holland!

The beat is characterised by the houses on the South side that back onto the river. Relationships with the frontager residents have generally been cordial, but there have been a few notable exceptions over the last 70 years.

It was here that one house owner built a boat slip and moored his boat thus starting the dispute with the landlord that precipitated the formation of the Club (see Chapter One).

In the fifties, members were permitted to fish from both banks of the Tonford beats, but not from private gardens without the permission of the occupiers. Members had the right to walk along both banks within four feet of the water's edge, and river frontagers were obliged to stop their boundary fences 10 feet from the water to allow access to anglers and River Board workers. This obligation is thought to remain, though there is little, if any, compliance.

In the early nineteen sixties, the land along Hassall Reach started to be developed. This is named after the poet Christopher Hassall of Tonford Manor, the nearby moated manor house. At the time, the Club had the use of two rented parcels of land for car parking, one on each side of Tonford Lane, but feared it might lose these to development. It was decided to try and purchase a suitable parking plot, but none could be found.

Meanwhile, building started along Hassall Reach. In 1966, one of the new bungalow owners took exception to parking by Club members on one of the plots that the Club rented from a Mr Peebles and objected to them walking along the riverbank at the rear of his new bungalow. He blocked the right of way to the parking land and fenced his property right up to the water's edge. Bizarrely, he also interfered with fishing by a new member, Mrs Paula Fowler, by persistently entering the water with his son and splashing around her to put the fish down. The Club took this interference with its access to the river very seriously and instructed the Club's solicitors Coates, Allbutt, and Taylor to seek a High Court injunction to enforce its rights. The same action was taken against several frontagers who would not remove walls and fences that had been constructed down to the water's edge. Nevertheless, these infringements are universal today!

In 1996, another frontager, who ignorantly claimed riparian rights, was responsible for 'verbal and nuisance attacks' on members fishing opposite his cottage. More recently, in 2014, the new owner of a house at the top of the beat thought it acceptable to throw stones at a member who was wading opposite his garden. A visit from the police and a warning put him right.

Lower Tonford

The Lower Tonford beat starts at the junction with the entrance to the curious semi-circular cutting that surrounds what is today eponymously known to members as 'the donkey field'. Club member Antony Wynn told me the perhaps apocryphal tale that some years ago the farmer who owned this field desperately wanted to fish the river and applied to join the Club (or a predecessor) but he was repeatedly turned down, it was suggested, because of his social status and bearing. He therefore took the matter into his own hands and dug the cutting to provide his own private beat on the Great Stour!

There was at one time a plank bridge across the main river here but its whereabouts and fate are not known.

The beat continues down under the A2 bridge, past the new footbridge at the rear of the retail park to the junction with the feeder drain on the North side.

A Beautiful Day at Lower Tonford

When the A2 Canterbury bypass was first mooted, one of the proposed routes would have placed the flyover near the Milton Road Bridge. It was inevitable that it would cross the Tonford beat somewhere. When the final route was selected, the Club was a statutory consultee in the Compulsory Purchase Order proceedings because it had rights over part of the land. In 1977 and 1978, seeing the construction of the road as inevitable, and without any grounds for a claim, the Club chose not to oppose it. It merely awaited financial compensation…which apparently went not to the Club but to the riparian owner! The chosen location certainly has had less impact on the Club's fishing than the other routes might have had.

The A2 flyover crosses the Club's water in the Thanington Court Farm area. Thanington Court is a mainly 17th Century Grade 2 Listed Building, though some parts are medieval. It was owned and occupied by Mr Lew Schwarz, a Club Committee member for several years. He won the Kendrick Cup in 1975. Mr and Mrs Schwarz hosted Committee meetings and a Club social event at the house, and they even allowed Club members to park their cars on their land.

Club Beat Names: Past and Present

	BEAT NAMES	
Originally	**Then**	**Present**
	Deanery	Upper Deanery
		Lower Deanery
	Paper Mill	
	Horton	Upper Horton
		Lower Horton
	The Top Water	Milton
Milton Bridge	Milton Pool	Upper Tonford
Weir Pool	Tolputt's Meadow	
Ford/Roadside Stretch	Roadside Trees	
Thatched House Garden		
Double Fence	Garden Backs	Middle Tonford
Tonford Bridge	Upper Tonford Reach	
Cattle Drink/Canal Stretch	Mill's Reach	Lower Tonford
Fast water	Vicarage Reach	
Plank Bridge	Wood's Shades	
Bottom Boundary	Lower Meadow	

Chapter Four

Fish, Fishing, Flies and Weeds

Fish!

The length of the River Great Stour fished by the Club has had a resident population of wild brown trout, coarse fish including chub, dace, roach, pike, perch, minnows, and eels plus a small run of sea trout and, if it is to be believed, a very small run of salmon. Until 1980, at least, bream were prevalent between Chartham Paper Mill and the City boundary.

Since before the foundation of the Club, the resident trout population has been supplemented by stocking with brown trout to provide sport, and to take angling pressure off the wild trout. Since 2010, the stocked fish have all been infertile triploids to avoid risking the genetic integrity of the wild trout population. Coarse fish have been systematically removed for transfer to other Clubs' waters. Initially this was by netting and later by electro-fishing. Bailiffs and some trusted local coarse fishers have been allowed to fish for pike on the condition that any caught are 'rehoused' elsewhere.

The Club has the right to fish for coarse fish outside the trout season and has considered selling day tickets to coarse anglers but has never done so. Initially, this was because AVM Fraser was opposed to it, and later because it was felt that it would be impossible to police without a full-time bailiff.

In 1951, a major concern was to clear the river of coarse fish and improve the surface fly life. Chairman Harry Orr, a biologist, firmly believed that one of the reasons that the trout were feeding on the bottom and not showing on the surface was an excess of minnows and insufficient 'attractive surface fly'. So, it was resolved to clear the water of coarse fish, including minnows, and introduce more fly life. It was possible at that time to purchase fly ova from fish suppliers. In 1954 the Club decided to use fly boards too, and they have been tried several times since, most recently in 2006, but theft and vandalism has been a problem and the boards have had to be chained down.

While members have been divided about the retention of chub (the river still holds many fine examples up to 5lbs) the need to remove pike has been consistently and unanimously accepted. For some reason, the Great Stour has always held an exceptionally large population of pike. For several years, the Club set pike traps by Milton Bridge. The first electro-fishing took place in 1956. A 'fine head of trout from 3lbs down' was found above Milton Bridge on AVM Fraser's personal beat, but, below the bridge on Club water only a few trout, a few dace and 12 pike were found. The 12 pike were held in a tank pending transport to another water when, becoming a little stressed, the 12 pike vomited 18 trout. Pike with trout in their mouths were caught during electro-fishing in 1963, and some taken that day for the table were found to have trout inside them. Perhaps one Club member is at least partly correct when he refers to the Club's periodic stocking with trout as 'feeding the pike'.

Electro-fishing became an annual event until 1961 and each time pike were removed. After a lull in reports of pike and after it had caused some injuries to trout the year before, the Club declined electro-fishing in 1962. The Chairman was uncertain that this was the right decision when he heard that 170 pike had been removed from the river above the Club's beat. The following year the Club reversed its decision and 26 pike averaging 5lbs were removed from the Tonford stretch of the river.

Pike of over 10lbs are not uncommon on the Club beats. A 12lbs pike was caught by electro-fishing in 1985. A pike estimated at 15lbs was caught at the Deanery in 2017 and monsters of 23 and 19.5lbs were caught near the Milton road-bridge in 2018; all were promptly 'rehoused' in a coarse fishing lake. In 2017 Dr Jack Cohen was playing a trout when a large pike took it, and he managed to land both!

Mr Iain McDonald, a Club bailiff, with a pike from Milton

While many anglers find salmon and sea trout a mysterious and exciting quarry, when in December 1956 a number of sea trout were found during electro-fishing, Chairman Harry Orr, ever a brown trout purist, referred to them as a 'doubtful asset'. He felt that while they might provide good sport and a possible extension of the season, their spawning would disturb the redds and brown trout breeding. He believed that if the season were to be extended so that members could target sea trout, it would risk the capture of gravid brown trout. Today we know that sea trout, being of the same species, breed with resident brown trout and are important contributors to a river's brown trout population. Why some brown trout decide to migrate to the sea or estuaries, taking all the extra risks that migration entails, remains a mystery, though the scientific evidence suggests a strong genetic component, together with a quest for better feeding opportunities.

Negative feelings about sea trout showed again in 1958 when concern was expressed that the Kent River Board (KRB) was constructing fish ladders at Mill Weir in Canterbury. That year three salmon kelts were found in the river, one in Canterbury, one below Tonford bridge and one just above Milton bridge. When the KRB formally consulted the Club for its views on salmon and sea trout, the Committee was generally opposed to the encouragement of migratory fish. It decided to seek members' views at the AGM. The Committee referred to the lease and the Club's own Rules, both of which were directed to dry fly fishing for brown trout. Members were told that the migratory fish would reach the Club's waters after the season had closed and so fishing for them would require a change of rules and in any event could endanger spawning brown trout and their redds. Fishing for the migratory fish would involve wet flies, and a member fishing downstream might spoil the fishing of a member fishing upstream for brown trout. The meeting decided to tell the KRB that members were not happy with the encouragement of migratory fish but would be happy to receive a stocking of brown trout. An underlying argument was that if the presence of migratory fish became known, it might drive up the value of the fishery and the rent.

The Great Stour is still listed by the North Atlantic Salmon Conservation Organization as having a salmon population, but recent evidence is sparse. Two salmon were found on the Club's water during electro-fishing in 1960: a cock above Milton Bridge and a gravid hen at the bottom of the Tonford beat. In 1963 three salmon and two sea trout were released after electro-fishing. Two salmon kelts were released during the 1965 electro-fishing, and a 'big sea trout' was spotted at lower Tonford. A major electro-fishing exercise by the Southern Water Authority Area (SWA) Fisheries Inspector in 1980 revealed 'very good numbers of sea trout up to 8 or 10lbs below Chartham Paper Mill and the occasional fish up to 3 or 4 lbs higher up'. Salmon were spotted in 1982 above Milton Bridge and the SWA reported that many salmon were seen in the estuary that year where illegal netting was taking place. Thirty sea trout were seen in the river in 1983. The 1984 electro-fishing of the Club's water released numerous sea trout, two salmon of about 15lbs and a brown trout of 6 lbs, in addition to the coarse fish removed. Sea trout were again found by electro-fishing in 1997, and in 1998 17 sea trout weighing from 5-12lbs were caught during electro-fishing. Most recently, nine were released in 2019.

Former Club Treasurer John Dawson told me that he saw a huge salmon gracefully glide past him while he was wading above Tonford Bridge in the early 1990s. He recalls there being a well-known salmon lie at the start of the trees above Milton Bridge.

Electro-fishing In Progress

In 1995 the National Rivers Authority reported that Salmon had been recorded upstream of Canterbury. It attributed this to investment in sewage treatment and improvements in river water quality over the previous 20 years. The NRA built fish passes at obstructions to enable migratory fish to move up the river to spawning grounds and enable recolonisation of the catchment with salmon. However, the NRA's successor, the Environment Agency (EA), has received no reports of salmon anywhere on the river for 20 years. Steven Smith, local EA Fisheries and Biodiversity Officer, told me in 2020 that he believes that some reported salmon in the Stour may in fact have been sea trout. This may be so, but some were identified by experienced salmon and sea trout anglers. I am convinced that today most members would strongly approve of the presence of migratory fish and would support the efforts that are being made to preserve and enhance the sea trout run.

But it was not just migratory fish to which the Club was opposed for many years. On hearing that the CDAA were to introduce grayling, in 1960, the Committee stridently let it be known that they did not want grayling in the Tonford water. The grayling that the CDAA stocked downstream of the Club's beats unfortunately did not hold.

Attitudes to grayling have changed enormously over the last fifty years. Now most fly fishers welcome them. Stocking with grayling was raised again in 1999 and once more traditionalist Harry Orr led the opponents, claiming that grayling 'can overwhelm a river'. Mike Ross Browne, Chairman at the time, was also against grayling, stressing that 'this is historically a brown trout river.' The proposal failed. In 2015 the Club decided to seek the advice of the Grayling Trust and the Grayling Society and in 2017 members decided that they did indeed want to stock some grayling. However, this time it was one of the Club's landlords, the Stour Fishery Association, and the Environment Agency, which blocked the proposal.

While stocking with rainbow trout was formally rejected at the 1956 and 1969 AGMs, the Club's 'brown trout only' policy had to be relaxed when in April 1977 it proved impossible to source sufficient brown trout for stocking. One hundred rainbow trout of 13-14 inches were planted, thirty-nine of which were taken that year and a further two the following year. None were reported after that.

Trophy Trout

Captain C J Martin holds the Club record for a brown trout of 4lbs 12 oz caught in 2000, but we know from electro-fishing records that there have been bigger fish in the river.

The Best Fish Caught Each Season

In the early years of the Section and the Club, there were no competitions and no annual prizes. However, the members' catch returns reveal that the best fish caught were:

Date	Member	Weight of Best Fish
1951	H R Orr	2lb 2oz
1952	A Blackley Goble	2lb 12oz
1953	P B Holt	3lb 9oz
1954	H R Orr	2lb 5oz
1955	P B Holt	2lb 12oz
1956	J L Cooke	2lb 12oz

The Kendrick Cup

At the Annual General Meeting held on 12 April 1957, a suggestion was made that some part of the Club's water should be named in memory of Mr Thomas Luson Kendrick, a Folkestone solicitor. Kendrick had been a 'trusted friend and wise counsellor of the Club since its beginning.' It was noted that a favourite spot of Mr Kendrick was 'at the bottom of Tolputt's Meadow, top of the roadside trees' i.e., at the bottom of the current Milton car park field. The AGM agreed unanimously that in future it should be known as *Kendrick's Corner*. Members were invited to subscribe to a silver trophy, to be named after Mr Kendrick that would be awarded to the member who caught the heaviest fish of the season. A silver cup was subsequently purchased - at 'an absurdly high price', according to the Committee Minutes!

The Cup has not been awarded every year. The winners are shown in the following table.

Date	Winner	Weight of Season's Best Fish
1957 C	C W Morris	3lb 12oz
1958 C	A J Parrott	2lb 14oz
1959 C	C W Morris	3lb 3oz
1960 C	H R Orr	2lb 9oz
1961 C	P Vickers	2lb 12oz
1962 C	P Vickers	2lb 2oz
1963 C	P Vickers	2lb 3oz
1964 C	J B Verbi	2lb 4oz
1965 C	H A Clapham	1lb 14oz
1966 C	A D Harrison	1lb 14oz
1967 C	P H B Holt	2lb 4oz
1968	N H Steed	2lb 4oz
1969	A J Parrott	Not recorded
1970	No record of an award	
1971	No record of an award	
1972	No record of an award	
1973	No record of an award	1lb 8oz
1974	No record of an award	1lb 5oz
1975	L Schwarz	2lb. 12oz

Year	Name	Weight
1976	Not recorded	1lb 12oz
1977	No record of an award	
1978	H R Orr	2lb. 3oz
1979	P E Cooke	1lb. 15oz
1980	H R Orr	3lb. 0oz
1981	C H T Bond / R B Tuttle	2lb 5oz
1982 C	N H Steed	2ib 4oz
1983 C	H R Orr	2lb 4oz
1984 C	N H Steed	2lb 5oz
1985 C	M R Goodliff	3lb 2oz
1986 C	M Ross Browne	3lb 4oz
1987 C	M R Goodliff	2lb 8oz
1988 C	Capt. C J Martin	2lb 15oz
1989	Capt. C J Martin	2lb 7oz
1990 C	N Williams	3lb 8oz
1991 C	H R Orr	3lb 0oz
1992 C	C J Martin	2lb 7oz
1993	R Godfrey-Faussett	2lb 6oz
1994	Capt. C J Martin	2lb 1oz
1995	No award was made	
1996 C	J B Cohen / C W B Jardine	2lb 6oz
1997 C	N Denne	3lb 2oz
1998 C	J B Cohen / J Lindsay	3lb 4oz
1999 C	B C Skeats	3lb 0oz
2000 C	Capt. C J Martin	4lb 12oz (Club Record)

2001	No award was made	
2002 C	J B Cohen	3lb 8oz
2003 C	M N O'Sullivan	2lbs 11oz
2004	M N O'Sullivan	3lb 0oz
2005	I Brett	Not recorded
2006	No record of an award	
2007	J C Dawson	3lbs 10oz
2008	No record of an award	3lbs 8oz
2009	No record of an award	
2010 C	J C Dawson	3lbs 10oz
2011 C	J B Cohen	3lb 0oz
2012 C	I Pattenden	3lb 0oz
2013	No Award Made	
2014 C	I Pattenden	2lb 15oz
2015	Y Chastang	49cm (c3lbs)
2016	No award was made	
2017	No award was made	
2018	No award was made	3lbs 0oz
2019	No award was made	

C = Engraved on the Cup

These awards are today made by reference to members' own catch returns, so they rely very much on trust. However, in the early years, nearly all trout were killed for the table and could readily be weighed. From 1957 to 1963 a set of weighing scales was provided by the Club in a hut on land at Hassall Reach held by Mr Mills the bailiff, for which the Club paid him a nominal rent. All members were provided with a key to this hut, and they were permitted to leave their tackle there and to park nearby on Mills' land. Mr Mills was a Club bailiff for over thirty years. The original intention was that the hut would also contain a 'game book' for catch returns and an 'In/Out' board to give an indication of how many members were already fishing the water (only 8 members were allowed to fish any one time), but members complained that this would be an interference with their freedom and the proposals were dropped. In recent years when most trout have been quickly and safely returned, their weight has been estimated.

Fishing

When the Section was formed in 1951, the Rules specified 'the object of the Section is to develop and enjoy angling for trout with an artificial dry fly'. The Rules further reinforced that 'the only bait to be used on the water shall be the artificial dry fly.' This was the traditional, classic, way to fly fish for trout. Fishing a nymph and casting downstream were anathema to the early denizens of the sport.

Nationally, earlier in the century, there had been a major discourse in the fly-fishing world about the 'acceptability' of nymph fishing and therefore it was inevitable that eventually there would be pressure from members for the Club to permit the use of a nymph. The rules were duly changed, but qualified: 'the nymph shall only be fished upstream.' Particularly in the days of Harry Orr's chairmanship, the traditional concept of fly fishing was fiercely preserved. Thirty years later at the 1981 AGM Dr Orr found it necessary to remind members that nymph fishing must (underlined in the minutes) be upstream. He repeated it a year later, adding that wet flies were not allowed. John Dawson remembers being challenged by Harry Orr in the 1990s for allegedly fishing a nymph!

Some members' conservative attitude to fly fishing methods was highlighted in 1958 when a change to the byelaws was proposed to ban the 'New Zealand method' or 'klink and dink' as it is sometimes now known. In this method a nymph is suspended from the hook of a dry fly. The dry fly acts as both an attractor and an indicator. 'The floating fly is virtually a float!' complained an outraged Mr Vickers. Nevertheless, the proposed ban was rejected since 'the method is recommended by accepted authorities.'

With eight members fishing 2000 yards of river at Tonford and nearly all fish being taken, there were concerns that it might be over-fished. The finger was pointed at Harry Orr, the Chairman, who often brought his brother or his students as guests. Orr had taken 44 fish in 1954 and 39 in 1955. Orr bristled at the suggestion! A proposal to limit members to 10 days fishing per month was defeated, but it was agreed that the Rules should be amended to impose a maximum catch (taken or not) of four fish over the size limit per day and six per week.

The issue was raised again in October 1957 when a fellow member complained that 'Mr Morris has been fishing too much'. Morris took 64 fish that year and won the Kendrick Cup for a fish of 3lbs 12oz. The Committee decided that 'this is a fishing Club, and a member is entitled to use it for fishing.' Nevertheless, Harry Orr (who had taken 41!) agreed to have a quiet word with Mr Morris to suggest that 'moderation might improve the feeling in the Club.' The following year Morris took 45 and Orr 43!

Over the years Club rules have been modified so that today, while dry fly and upstream nymph are still *de rigueur*, 'after 1st September a single hook wet fly may be used in the pursuit of migratory fish. The use of barbless hooks is to be encouraged and no hook larger than a size 8 may be used.'

The Author Hooks a Rising Trout at the Deanery

In the early days, all fish over 12 inches were taken for the table whereas today most members fish only 'catch and release' or perhaps they might take an occasional fish. Catch and release was first formally considered by the Club in 1988. The matter was left to individual member's discretion, provided that there would be minimal handling of any fish to be released and unhooking takes place in the water. The recommendations to use barbless hooks and 'no netting out of the water' followed in 1989.

The catch limit remains: 'No member shall catch more than four trout above the minimum size limit per day and may kill no more than six trout per week', but it has been modified to allow catch and release after this limit has been reached: 'A member having caught this latter limit may continue to fish but must use a barbless hook.'

A Member Fishes the Milton Beat

Flies

Today, Club members are required to submit an annual catch return with an indication of where each fish was caught and its weight. Initially, the Club catch returns, then known as the 'Game Book', also required the member to state the type of fly. These 'game books' were meticulously analysed and collated by Secretary Walter Smith during his 15-year tenure. Unfortunately, there are no such records for subsequent years. In his annual reports over 40 years, Chairman Harry Orr would generally comment on the natural flies present and artificial flies used during the year. He also gave a useful summary after thirty years in the post. So, at least for the Tonford stretch, there is an excellent record of the flies that were successfully used over a period of 40 years. This tells us which natural flies were prevalent over the seasons of that period. It may merely tell us which artificial flies were fashionable at the time - as only flies that are selected by the angler can be successful!

From these records we can make an overall summary:

Early Season (April and May): Mayfly (to 1958), Hares Ear, Blue Wing Olive, Dark Olives

Mid-Season (June and July): Mayfly (to 1958), Sedge, Blue Wing Olive, Sherry Spinner

Late Season (August and September): Pheasant Tail Nymphs, Sedge, Red/Sherry/Rusty Spinners

Mayflies were prevalent on the Tonford Stretch when the Club and Section were founded, but then declined and had disappeared by 1963. Sedges became less numerous too. A few Mayflies were seen in 1988 and they had become more numerous again by 1994, but despite a good year in 2005 have never been as prominent again at Tonford. When the Club took the Deanery beat in 2004 members were pleasantly surprised by its good Mayfly hatch and that beat continues to produce good Mayfly numbers to this day. The perceived problem in 2020 was lots of mayflies but few rises! Former Club secretary Anthony Pound is convinced that these days the elevated water temperature is a contributary factor.

A Tonford Mayfly Dun (Ephemera danica)

Trout fishers always wish for more surface fly action and that has certainly been the case at Tonford. In the late 1950s and early 1960s, the Club experimented with introducing flies, purchasing caddis ova from fish suppliers, but without success. Fly boards have proved useful but have suffered from vandalism and theft.

Weeds

Weeds have been a perennial problem. Weed growth is prolific in July and August, exacerbated by reduced flow and high levels of nitrates and phosphates. When the Club was formed, weeds were cut periodically by the Kent River Board (KRB). The Committee preferred that patches should be left uncut to provide cover and food for the fish and lobbied the KRB for longitudinal 'weed islands' to be left and less radical cutting generally. The KRB responded positively and invited the Club to produce a scheme of improvements including groynes and winter fish shelter. Cutting in autumn was discouraged because it reduced the stock of food for overwintering fish, but, to the Committee's dismay, the KRB cut weed in September 1956 without even giving prior notice. After some discourse with the KRB, the Committee was able to report that the 1957 weed cutting was the best ever for fish conservation. As recently as 2015 the weeds were cut from the Corn Mill to Tonford by the Environment Agency weed cutting boat. More recently, the Club has had to rely on the hard work of volunteer members to keep the river fishable in July and August.

A Weed Cutting Party

Chapter Five

Pollution, Poaching and Boating

Pollution

In 1962, in an article in *The Field*, member Mr Donald Dougall commented about the Club's stretch of the Great Stour that 'it suffers less from pollution than from abstraction'. To some extent that remains true nearly sixty years later, but the water has been and remains affected by both point-source and non-point sources of pollution. While it is, thankfully, largely untouched by pollution from heavy industry, diffuse 'invisible' non-point sources include the run-off and percolation of agricultural and horticultural pesticides, herbicides, and fertilisers. Point sources include the outfall from several sewage treatment plants. The impact of all pollutants is exacerbated by the raised concentrations that inevitably follow water abstraction, particularly in dry summers.

The first recorded pollution incident during the Club's tenure of the Tonford stretch was a cesspool that overflowed into the river in 1960. This was soon dealt with by Bridge Blean Rural District Council. Chronic sewage pollution was suspected in 1964 when the Club noted excessive growth of 'flannel weed' and silting up of weeds, reed beds and former gravel beds. Flannel weed, more often referred to as blanket weed, is a mat of filamentous algae. It can be an indicator of nitrate and/or phosphate pollution. When this was raised with officers of the Kent River Board, they replied that 'a new sewage works is now in operation at Ashford', thus intimating both the source and their prospective solution of the problem. Nevertheless, it was decided to keep a close watch, as the problems seemed to persist after the new sewage works came into operation. Indeed, heavy blanket-weed growth remains a problem today.

But it was not just blanket-weed and silt; the following year members noted that crayfish and minnows had disappeared from the Tonford stretch, and the members' annual catch returns had been in decline for 5 years. Chairman Harry Orr, a biologist, also believed that the trout had become sluggish, and he postulated that a pollutant with a high biological oxygen demand was to blame, in addition to the lack of rainfall and water abstraction. It was hoped that stocking with 450 fresh fish might form the nucleus of the fishery's recovery.

In 2020, a crayfish survey was carried out by the Kentish Stour Countryside Partnership for the Environment Agency on the Club's water. They put out and monitored 30 traps, but no crayfish were found. Chalkstreams are generally regarded as the ideal habitat for the species, and the river above Chilham was once considered the best crayfish habitat in the country, so the sustained complete loss of the crayfish population from the Club's water (without colonisation by alien crayfish) is certainly a concern. Reference to the Environment Agency Technical Report would suggest four possible causes: reduced flow due to abstraction; sewage works effluent; agricultural pollution from sheep dip chemicals, and field run-off. Recent research by the Salmon and Trout Association would suggest that the decline of mayflies in the UK as a whole is due to sewage pollution and phosphates and fine sediment run-off from farmed fields.

While Orr suspected sewage pollution, he regarded water abstraction as the greatest threat. According to contemporary Club Minutes, the Mid Kent Water Company already extracted

3 million gallons a day from under the Stour Valley and in 1965 it advertised its intention to extract a further 6 million gallons a day (mgd) making a total of 9 mgd from the subsoil between Godmersham and Chartham. Worryingly, the Company had the support of the Kent River Authority in its application to the Minister for approval, so it would be very difficult to successfully oppose it.

There was already a bore hole at Milton/Thannington, but the Club learned that as part of its plan, the Mid Kent Water Company was proposing to sink two further bore holes at Horton. This was to enable them to pump 'compensation water' into the river if the summer flow at the Horton gauging weir should fall below 23 mgd. This set off alarm bells at the Club, for the normal summer low was 30 mgd and indeed the flow had had only fallen below 23 mgd on one exceptional occasion in twenty years. Was a major reduction in flow envisaged? Would the river have even less clean water to dilute any pollutants? The Club resolved to make a formal objection to the Minister, and a member, Mr Ross, raised the issue at a meeting of the Kent River Authority.

Then the SFA informed the Club that Mid Kent Water had increased its demand to 20 mgd! The SFA asked the club and the CDAA to join with them to vigorously oppose this plan which had the potential to ruin the river as a trout fishery. The Club agreed to contribute to the cost of counsel, a biologist, and a consultant water engineer; indeed, at its AGM, the general membership doubled the amount originally proposed by the Committee, though the brunt was still borne by the SFA. The three clubs sought the support of the Anglers Cooperative Association (now known as 'Fish Legal') in their fight. While the Minister subsequently agreed to only half of the water company's demand, it was not a victory for the three clubs, for at 10 mgd the volume of permitted abstraction was over three times the previous amount, and it would inevitably adversely affect the character of the river. One might be forgiven for thinking that Mid Kent Water's demand was increased to 20 mgd to enable the Minister to make a politically acceptable compromise.

Today, South East Water, which has succeeded Mid Kent Water, has licences to abstract water at four locations in the Stour Valley: Godmersham; Chilham and Chartham (though water is only abstracted at Chilham); Howfield (this is probably the 'Milton' site referred to above), and Thannington. South East Water told me that today it is licenced to abstract 13.64 million litres a day (just over 3 mgd) of ground water from Chilham at all times and no matter how low the river falls, without the need to compensate the river. Only if this Chilham abstraction limit is exceeded (which they claim never happens) must it pass compensation water into the river during low river flows. Only the Chilham licence is linked to river flow in this way, it says.

While a report earlier in the year from biologist Dr Margaret Browne had found the river to be in good health, in November 1966 floods brought pollution into the Stour and dead trout were found on the Tonford stretch, at Chilham and in the city reaches. It was thought that the fish had been poisoned in SFA water (i.e., above Milton) and that subsequent dilution downstream had protected the river at Tonford. Nevertheless, the club felt it necessary to increase stocking to compensate.

Pollution brought by heavy floods in 1977 resulted in losses of both trout and sea trout. The source was never identified but it was thought to be above the Milton Bridge.

Chairman Harry Orr told the 1977 AGM that the river had a high concentration of nitrates and phosphates, and this resulted in excessive weed growth. He said that this was due to sewage pollution and the run-off of agricultural chemicals.

In 1985 Brett Ltd caused much concern in the Club when they applied for permission to discharge gravel working effluent directly into the river. Fortunately, they subsequently withdrew their application.

During a spell of very cold weather in early 1987, the sewage works at Ashford was out of action for several days with the result that untreated effluent found its way into the river turning the water a deep red colour. A vast number of fish were killed, mainly on SFA water upstream of the Club's length. The SWA donated some fish in the 6-10 inches range 'as a gesture of good will.'

In 1997 the river was polluted with sewage from a farm near the railway embankment. In June, the river turned green for several hours, probably because of an algal bloom, but with no apparent lasting consequences.

The same year, polluting run-off, described as 'foul and silt-laden', from Brett's works entered the river on several occasions upstream of Milton Bridge. The silt was evident well downstream and allegedly killed invertebrates and smothered weeds. Chairman at the time, Dr Jack Cohen, told me that he had to call out the Environment Agency on several occasions, with the result that operations at Brett Ltd were stopped, and in 1998 Brett Ltd was prosecuted by the EA. I contacted Bretts for their corroboration, but without any response.

Under The Water Framework Directive, in 2019 the overall classification of the river between Wye and the A2, which includes the whole of the Club's water, was 'moderate'. Ecological quality was categorised as 'moderate' and chemical quality as 'fail.' The Environment Agency confirmed that pollution from rural areas and from wastewater prevented the river achieving 'good' status

In recent years weed growth, especially blanket-weed, has been excessive with some lengths of river becoming completely unfishable in July and August. Nitrate and phosphate from agriculture and sewage effluent continue to be the likely culprits. The Club has encouraged local universities and conservation groups to undertake studies of the problem, with the offer of some financial support.

Poaching

The problem of poaching was raised at the Section's very first meeting in 1951 and it remains an issue today. It has become much more of a problem since access to the Club's water was encouraged and readily facilitated by the opening of the Great Stour Way in 2011.

While there have been stories of organised gangs netting trout at Lower Tonford and The Deanery, the club feels that some of the current loss of trout is also at the hands of individuals and small groups. Members occasionally come across individual anglers in broad daylight, even some with fly tackle,

Poachers Spinning at the Deanery

who despite general knowledge and the many signs erected by the club, plead ignorance of the necessity for a licence and Club membership. More worrying and difficult to address has been the clandestine poaching during the hours of darkness and early morning that has been reported by residents. Some poachers angle with spinners and plugs, others set baited night lines. A 21st century poaching practice is 'cement bagging' whereby a bag of cement is cut with a knife and thrown into the river. The cement powder seeps into the water leaving the Club's trout on the surface, apparently asphyxiated but not poisoned and able to be readily gathered up lower downstream. John Dawson recalls that in a similar way in the 1990s, poachers threw fire extinguishers into the water to de-oxygenate a length of the river.

The problem has been considered many times, legal opinion has been sought, there has been a discourse with the local police and poachers have been caught red-handed, yet there does not seem to have been a single prosecution of a poacher during the life of the Club. The Club's Minutes even name Mr Griffiths and Mr Wiffin as poachers, but neither was prosecuted. Even a single prosecution would surely have gone a long way towards getting the message across.

In the nineteen-sixties part-time club bailiff Mr Pageham, a local farm manager, would patrol the river with his shotgun over his arm. This helped to ensure that he was, according to Club records, 'effective in his dealings with local toughs.' However effective it might have been, this would not be advocated today!

In the 1980s, PCs from Chartham Police Station would speak at the Club's AGMs. They stressed that poachers can be violent, and members should not intervene personally but should take evidence and report the matter to the police. Members were told that there were 16 'police actions' against poachers in 1980, but there were no prosecutions.

In 2005 poachers were caught in the act by bailiff Mr Tony Cornwall who seized tackle worth £350. The police were called, and evidence was taken, but again no prosecution resulted. A week later the bare-faced poachers emailed to ask for their tackle back! Without the matter going to court, in law the tackle would have to be handed over. The Club's clever response was that the tackle would be delivered to the poachers if they would just give their names and addresses. They never did, of course.

Poaching was again a big issue in 2007. The Chairman sent out frequent emails to update members. The bailiffs complained that they received no support from the police.

The river was heavily poached on several occasions in 2010. Four poachers were caught at Horton, but no action was taken by the police. Another poacher was caught with 9 trout on the bank, but once again no prosecution was brought. Poachers were also caught in 2011. Again, in 2013, Club bailiffs were called out on several occasions to deal with poachers. Two Police Community Support Officers attended one incident and tackle was seized, but as usual there were no prosecutions. At the time, a member who was a senior police officer commented that 'too few people have a proper understanding of where the law stands and what can be done. It is very disappointing that the police did not exercise the power of arrest at the time since then there would have been the requirement upon them to put together a case. The seized equipment would have become evidence in a criminal case which may have resulted in the court ordering forfeiture and imposing a penalty.'

Club member Mr Laurie Day researched and produced a paper for the Club on the law relating to poaching, but at the time the Club felt that it could not rely on the law or for the authorities to take the matter seriously, so it tried alternative proactive approaches. Mr Tony Cornwall, a former prison officer, visited local farms to give talks to European farm workers who might not understand that in the UK freshwater fishing generally requires both a licence and a permit. He also successfully ran fishing contests for local children in Chartham and tried to re-establish links with the local police. He developed a network of supportive dog walkers and cyclists who would contact him with information. In 2010, the Club formally put on record its appreciation of Tony Cornwall's efforts. The Club continues to put up 'Private Fishing' signs as vandalism continually takes its toll on them.

In 2019 and 2020, under new Chairman Mr Gary Lagdon, the Club adopted several measures to strengthen its position against poaching. It displayed yet more signs to identify the Club water and prohibit illegal fishing; some being multilingual in recognition of the area's multinational agricultural workforce. It invited a representative of the Angling Trust to the 2020 AGM to make a short presentation on the importance of properly reporting incidents for maximum effect with the enforcement authorities. It produced new bailiff appointment documentation and guidelines on procedures for reporting poaching. It has tried CCTV monitoring of poaching hotspots, but the cameras were stolen!

New bailiffs will be trained under the Angling Trust Voluntary Bailiff Scheme with an emphasis on reporting and working with the Kentish Stour Countryside Partnership river-wardens, the Environment Agency, and Rural Police. With more active reporting, poaching in 2021 seems even more evident than in previous years and, as I write, it remains to be seen whether the new measures will be effective. One would hope for more support from the rural police and EA fisheries enforcement.

Current policy when young anglers are caught poaching on Club waters is to direct them to the free fishing below the Club water. When appropriate, young anglers may be persuaded to become a member and they may even be offered free fly-fishing tuition.

Not all the poachers on Club waters are human. In 1986 a problem with mink taking fish became evident. Sightings of 'otters' around this time were almost certainly of mink. The Club purchased mink traps and one mink was caught. Two more were caught in 1988 and after that none were seen on the river until 1996 when traps were set, though none were caught. Six were trapped in 1998, and there were no further sightings until 2011 when a mink was spotted feeding at Horton Weir.

Cormorants around the fishing lakes and river have become an increasing problem too, as they are protected by law, and despite several unsuccessful attempts by past secretary Mr Anthony Pound, the Club has not been successful in obtaining a licence to control them. Mr Pound found that there were too many administrative and technical hurdles placed in his path by the Environment Agency who seemed more eager to protect the invasive cormorants than the native brown trout. Currently the Club is allowed to merely scare them off and to provide refuges to offer protection to the fish. To this end, the Club would prefer that weed cutting should finish at the end of July as the weed provides a refuge for the fish. Unfortunately, the Environment Agency's use of a weed cutting boat in September is at odds with this natural and ecologically sound approach.

Acting on advice from the Angling Trust's cormorant expert, the Club is considering installing gabion baskets to provide additional fish sanctuary.

Boating, Canoeing and Bathing

Soon after the section was formed in 1951, members became bothered by unauthorised boating, particularly at weekends. One of the Club's first actions was to erect 'No Boating' and 'No Bathing' signs. Examination of AVM Fraser's legal title to the river confirmed that boats on the Club's water were trespassers. Members and the bailiff were asked to draw this to the attention of any unauthorised users and to gently

Inflatables Near Milton Bridge

request them to desist. It was recently confirmed that there is no public right of navigation to the West of the City boundary and indeed there used to be a boom across the river at this point to prevent the passage of boats upstream.

In 1954, the unauthorised boating and poaching by Mr Griffiths, as outlined in Chapter One, resulted in the formation of the Club. Griffiths had asked the Kent River Board for permission to put his boat on the river. They had replied that they 'had no objection to a boat'. On several occasions in the life of the Club, individuals and boating organisations would claim to have approached the police or the river authority and to have received permission. Of course, it is not within the police's or a river authority's purview to grant or deny permission to a boater to use a river. There is still widespread public ignorance of the legal position that prior permission must be obtained from the riparian owner.

The unauthorised stationing and use of a boat by Scott and Griggs, a local firm of fruit packers, was discovered in 1963. The firm was advised of the legal position and the boat was sold.

In 1964, the King's School Canoe Club claimed the right to use the Tonford stretch of the river, stating that they had 'police permission'. Once again, the Club sought legal advice and was advised that there is no general right of navigation on its private water. This was conveyed to the school 'in a friendly tone' in the hope that there would be no further trespass. In 1965 it was also necessary to write to the Canterbury Sea Scouts in the same way.

When the Deanery beat was added to the Club's water, the SFA, the Club's landlord and riparian owner, confirmed that while some of the residents of Riverside kept boats moored opposite their houses, they did not have boating or fishing rights on the river. Nevertheless, in 2008 boating on the Deanery beat made fishing impossible at times. The SFA, eager to compromise with canoeists, had previously agreed to allow British Canoe Union (BCU) members to use the river outside the game fishing season. Unfortunately, this agreement was often broken by canoeists and the sight of canoes on the water in the winter seemed to invite unauthorised use during the season, so in 2015, having an obligation to its landlord to protect his rights, the Club found it necessary to write to the

Bathers at the Deanery

BCU to cancel the arrangement. In the interests of good neighbour relations, the Club has so far not acted against use by Riverside residents, but it reserves the right to do so.

Trespass by canoeists and other boaters continued to a greater or lesser extent each year thereafter, and reached a head in 2020 when, during the pandemic 'lockdown', swimming, canoeing, paddleboarding and boating was rife throughout the Club's waters but particularly on the Deanery beats. This was most intense during a spell of hot weather that coincided with the closure of schools. Fishing in the mayfly season was impossible at times and generally unproductive due to the disturbance of the water.

One canoeing instructor was even spotted on several occasions using the Club's water near the Parish Road bridge for the purpose of giving lessons for a fee.

A Group of Illegal Canoeists at the Deanery Mill Pool

In July 2020, a canoe club advertised an outing from Chartham Village to Chartham Mill Pool for a £10 fee and invited participants to bring food and drink for a party on the private farmland at the mill pool. The farmer and occupiers of the houses overlooking the pool were outraged. Club members responded by turning out in numbers, forming a human chain across the river to block the passage of some 30 canoes.

Members Confronting Illegal Canoeists

Chairman Gary Lagdon, standing chest-deep in the water, calmly spoke with the leader of the group of canoeists and explained the legal position. The canoeists departed reluctantly but peacefully on that occasion, but the problem of unauthorised boating on the Club's private water remained, and later in the year large groups of canoeists were again seen trespassing on the Deanery beats.

Chapter Six

The Club and its Waters in the Media

We don't know if he ever fished the Club's stretch, but certainly the venerable Izaak Walton fished the Great Stour near Canterbury. In *The Compleat Angler* he writes of huge 'Fordidge trout', 'many of the bigness of salmon', which had distinctive white flesh. These would have been sea trout; 'Fordidge' being Fordwich.

In 1895, in an article in *The Field*, author E. T. Sachs also extolled the hidden virtues of the trout fishing on the Great Stour: 'we have at Chartham a preserved fly water of considerable excellence …under the protection of the Chartham Association'; the water below the city being at the time under the control of the Lower Stour Fishery Association and mainly a coarse fishery. Even in those times, there were problems with poachers and with bathers 'not so sparing as they might be in exhibitions of their nakedness'. Fortunately, today's bathers are usually more modest, though just as irksome.

In his book *Here and There a Lusty Trout*, T. A. Powell recalls his visits to the Great Stour during the air raids of the Second World War. Whenever he could, he would escape after his week's work at The Admiralty to his 'pied a terre' at Chilham, with an eye on the sky and an ear to the drone of enemy aircraft. After the early evening train journey from London, his first stop would be The Woolpack in Chilham, just before closing time, where no doubt he would plan the following day. His precious day off on the river would be followed by a reluctant journey behind blackout curtains back to Charing Cross Station.

In the first few years of its existence several 16mm films of the Club's activities were made by Treasurer Alexander Blackley Goble. These films were shown at AGMs and lent to the CDAA for the same purpose. It is not known what became of them. It would be wonderful to re-discover them and to relive those days.

Mr Bernard Venables MBE, noted fishing author and illustrator, and founder of the *Angling Times*, was the speaker at the CDAA Annual Dinner in April 1959. He was the TFFC's guest that day at Tonford. I hope that he had a good catch. Mr Venables is best remembered for his classic, inspirational, book *Mr Crabtree Goes Fishing* that has sold over 4 million copies. I have one on my shelf.

In April 1962, Mr Jack Hargreaves OBE, who was the speaker at the CDAA Annual Dinner, was invited to fish the Tonford water and film for his TV programme *Out of Town*. I do not think that the Tonford footage was used in any of his programmes, and I cannot find any record of his catch that day. The Committee had some misgivings about his visit because it believed that any form of advertisement of its water might enhance its value... and the rent.

Concerns that publicity might result in a rent increase and attract poachers, emerged again later that year when, in November, an article by member Mr Donald Dougall appeared in *The Field* magazine. Entitled *Trout on the Kentish Stour* its main premise was that the Tonford and SFA fishing was comparable with the Hampshire and Wiltshire chalkstreams, and indeed, offered the best dry-fly fishing in England. The publication of this article so upset the Committee that it 'reproved (scolded) Mr Dougall for the publicity given to our water' and Committee member 'Mr Cooke was so annoyed that he wrote personally to Mr Dougall. No acknowledgement was received'. I doubt that Dougall was quaking in his boots. Dougall's claims were surprising since the catch returns show that he took but six fish that year, when the Chairman took 37.

Mr Charles Jardine, the internationally celebrated artist, author, fishing instructor, photographer, and much more, was a member. He was the Club's Secretary from 1994 to 1996.

Chapter Seven

The Club Today

The Club continues to lease water at Tonford, Milton and The Deanery, and has a licence to use land near Milton Bridge as a car park. The current Chairman, Mr Gary Lagdon,

The Chairman With A Nice Wild Brownie

originally by profession an architect and project manager, runs an international fly-fishing guiding business. He has experience in river keeping and fisheries management. His expertise and practical support have proved invaluable to the Club and to individual members in recent years.

A Member Catches Her First Trout

Of course, it is the members that make a Club and in 2021, under the Chairman, the Secretary, Mr Neil Rogers, the Treasurer, Mr Simon Chandler, and the guidance of the Management Committee, membership has risen to nearly fifty. The Club encourages people of all ages to join and actively seeks to be inclusive and to extend its diversity.

River walks with the Chairman before the start of each season have helped to introduce prospective and new members to our water.

Members may share their rod with a friend or family member to help to introduce them to the passion and gentle art of fly fishing on a beautiful chalk stream. Members are also entitled to apply for up to 4 daily guest permits a year, at a small fee, to allow a friend or family member to fish along with them.

The Club now offers a limited number of permits to other Great Stour fly fishing clubs on a reciprocal basis. This not only gives our members access to more water, but it has fostered stronger ties with these other clubs, enabling them to present a unified lobby against threats to the river and its ecosystem.

The Club strives to protect the fragile environment of the Stour Valley from adverse and unsustainable developments, water abstraction and sewage discharges. In 2021 it joined with other local angling clubs (the Ford Mill Fishery, the Upper Stour Syndicate, the Stour Fishery Association and the Canterbury and District Angling Association) and Fish Legal to lobby against a proposed housing estate in Lenham. The Club considered that the local authority had not adequately considered the environmental impact, especially on fish, and on protected species and habitats in the River Stour downstream of the site.

The Club is constantly alert to threats to water quality and quantity and it participates in monthly surveys of aquatic invertebrates and water quality with The Kentish Stour Countryside Partnership, the Riverfly Database, the Our Stour project, Kent Wildlife, and other conservation bodies. Discussions are currently taking place with a local university that wishes to research water-borne parasites and fish movement along the river.

The Club is a member of The Angling Trust, which is a not-for-profit organisation that represents anglers, fighting for fish, fishing, and the environment.

The Club's bailiffs now include two who are accredited under the Angling Trust Voluntary Bailiff scheme. This links with both the Environment Agency and Rural Police and their databases and enables better reporting and response to incidents. Our members and the bailiffs also work with volunteer river wardens along the river, and with neighbours such as the Hambledon Marshes Trust, to better police and protect the river.

Over the season, the river is periodically stocked with triploid (neutered) brown trout to provide sport for members, together with a very large number of neutered fry and fingerlings that it is hoped will develop and consolidate to take angling pressure off the resident trout. Every effort is made to conserve and protect the river's natural resident population of brown trout.

Careful and considerate catch and release is practised by nearly all members, though the taking for the table of an occasional stock fish over the size limit is perfectly acceptable.

A Delivery of Stock Trout

Voluntary work parties are recruited from the membership to cut weed and for river keeping and conservation work. These events can forge friendships between members and help to develop an *esprit de corps*. The large turnout of members at very short notice in 2019, to form a human barrier across the river to challenge and educate a large party of unlawful canoeists, demonstrates the fine spirit of the membership.

The Club attempts to control the large population of pike by encouraging members to fly fish for pike outside the trout

A Work Party Takes A Well-Deserved Break

season, and by permitting a small number of selected local anglers to fish for pike with other angling methods, provided that any pike caught are taken for the table or are swiftly and humanely relocated to other waters.

In 2021 the Club decided to reinstate the office of Club President and Mr Mark Evans accepted the appointment. It was decided that 'The President's Trophy' would be awarded annually to the member who catches the most trout. 'The Kendrick Cup' continues to be awarded for the largest trout caught by a member each season.

The Tonford Fly Fishing Club has now provided fly fishing for trout on the beautiful River Great Stour for over 70 years, and long may it continue to do so!

Tonford Fly Fishing Club

TONFORD FLY FISHING CLUB

Rules and Byelaws adopted by an Extraordinary General Meeting on 15th December 1954

RULES

1. The club is called 'The Tonford Fly Fishing Club'.
2. The object of the club is to develop and enjoy angling in the River Stour in the vicinity of Tonford foot bridge. The pursuit of trout, with an artificial dry fly, shall have precedence, on the club's water, over any other form of angling.
3. Membership shall be restricted to 25 subscribing members. A member may not transfer his rights to any other person, except as provided in rule 9.
4. Applicants for membership shall be nominated by two existing members and approved by the committee of the club. The committee shall have the sole right to nominate persons from such applicants to vacancies in membership and to refuse to renew membership at their discretion.
5. A member of the club, fishing the water, shall show his membership card and bag to any official or other member on request. It shall moreover be deemed the duty of a member to challenge any person fishing the water, whom he does not know to be a member, to exchange scrutiny of membership cards and bags.
6. The entrance fee to the club shall be £5, payable on election to membership. The annual subscription shall be £10, payable in advance on 15th March, to cover the year commencing on the 1st April following.
7. No member shall fish until he has paid his subscription for the current year. The committee shall have the right, after giving notice, to terminate the membership of a member who has not paid his subscription by 15th March and offer his place to an applicant.
8. It shall be the duty of a member, before commencing to fish the water, to ensure that by so doing, he will not cause the limit of rods on the water laid down in the byelaws to be exceeded.
9. A member shall have the right to hand his rod to a friend who remains in his company, whether such friend be a member or no.
10. The landlord of the water, Air Vice Marshall H.H.M. Fraser, CB shall also be a member of the club and shall have the right to fish the water

himself and to nominate two other rods on any occasion. These three rods, if on the water, may be additional to the number allowed to members by the byelaws.

11. The committee shall have discretion to invite to fish the water as a guest of the club, persons who have been of service to the club or to the cause of angling generally. Such guests, not exceeding two at any one time, may be additional to the number allowed in the byelaws.

12. The only bait to be used on the water during the trout fishing season shall be an artificial dry fly or a nymph; the latter, if used, shall be fished upstream.

BYELAWS

1. Fishing Season
   For trout – 1st April to 30th September inclusive.
   For coarse fish – 1st October to 14th March inclusive.

2. Size Limits
   For trout – a minimum length of 12 inches overall.
   For coarse fish – as laid down by the Kent River Board.

3. Limit to Rods
   No more than eight members shall fish the water at any one time.

4. Number Limits
   No member shall take more that four trout per day nor more than six trout per week. A member having taken this limit shall stop fishing for the appropriate period.

5. Bait
   No member shall spin with a bait of an overall length of less than 3 inches.

6. Limits of the Water
   From Milton Bridge downstream, on the North West bank to the carrier entering the river next above the first viaduct; on the South East bank to

the Canterbury City boundary stone. Members may note that the water below these points is public.

7. Game Book

Every member shall keep a record of the trout he takes. At the end of the trout fishing season he shall inform the Secretary of the total number of trout he has killed during the season on the Tonford water, together with the weight or other particulars of any outstanding fish.

8. Legal

Our landlord owns the river bed and it becomes our duty as his tenants, to prevent trespass upon it or upon the water flowing over it. Our landlord and we, as his tenants, have a right of passage along both river banks, within four feet of the water, including passage through the bottom of private gardens, but no fishing may take place from private gardens without consent of the occupier. There is no public right of way along the river bank, but any person trespassing here would offend against the riparian owner and not against the owner or tenant of the fishery.

Miscellaneous

9. Reasonable wading is permitted, but members should exercise restraint in this matter.

10. The normal direction of progress when fishing with a dry fly is upstream. A member working downstream must yield to one working up, and a member walking downstream to a starting place must be careful not to disturb fish in the water above a member fishing below him. A member must not start fishing within 100 yards of another member without invitation.

11. Undersize fish must be returned to the water as soon as possible. The ideal is to unhook the fish in the water, but if it must be taken out, wet your hands before handling it, put it gently back into the water and let it swim out of your hand or net.

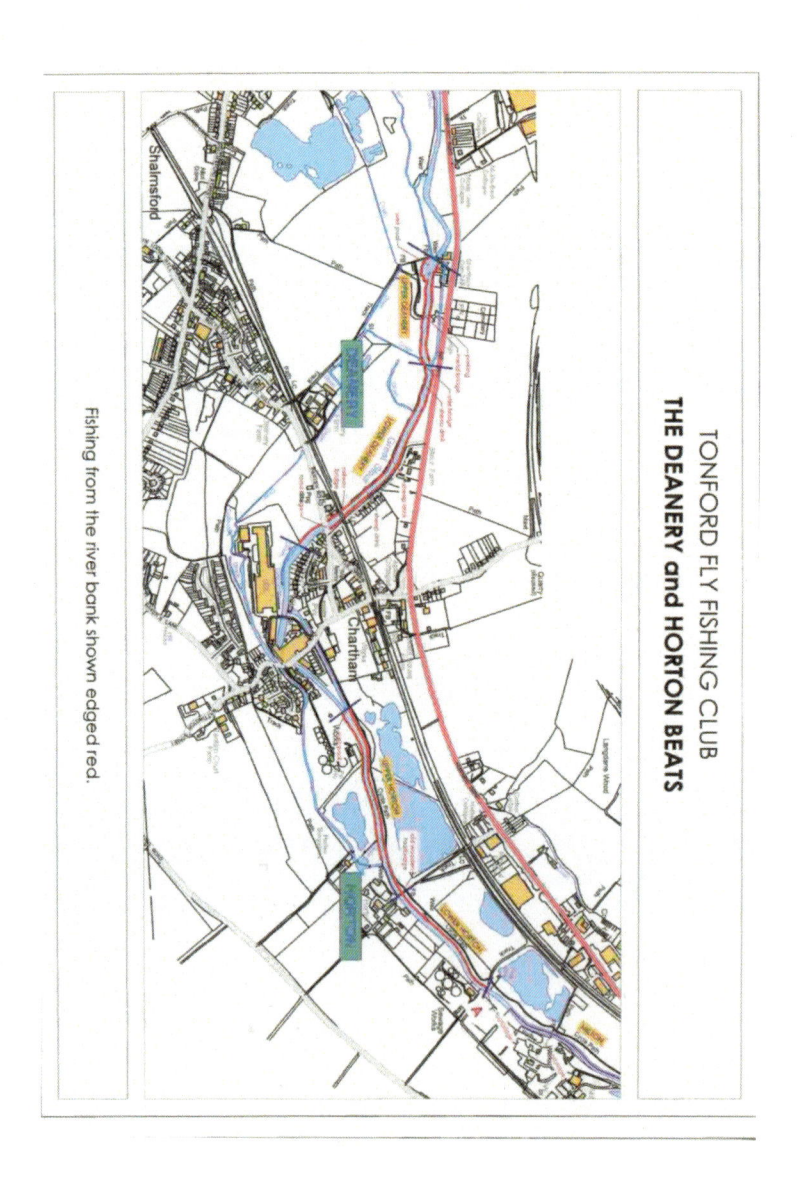

TONFORD FLY FISHING CLUB
THE DEANERY and HORTON BEATS

Fishing from the river bank shown edged red.

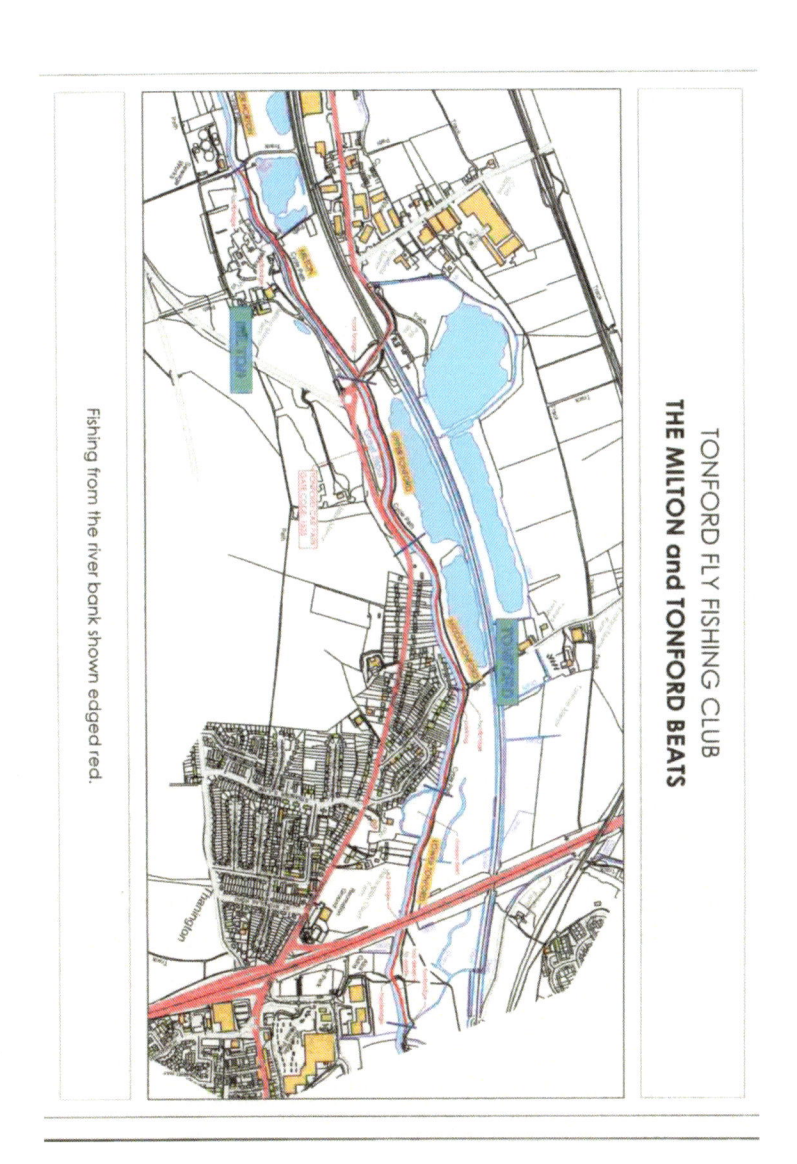

TONFORD FLY FISHING CLUB
THE MILTON and TONFORD BEATS

Fishing from the river bank shown edged red.

Source of Photographs

Air Vice-Marshall Hugh Fraser: Copyright the Royal Aero Club.

Dr Henry Orr: with thanks to Mid Kent College.

Cmdr. Alexander Blackley Goble: from ancestry.com.

Mr Michael Ross Browne: courtesy of Mrs Suzi Ross Browne.

Dr Jack Cohen: courtesy of Mrs Zeena Cohen.

Chartham Corn Mill 1930, and Upper Tonford Beat 1930: with kind permission of Octopus Books.

All other photographs were taken and donated by club members and bailiffs past and present.